MW00927861

GENO AURIEMMA

JOHN FREDRIC EVANS

Enslow Publishing
101 W. 23rd Street
Suite 240
New York, NY 10011
USA
enslow.com

Published in 2020 by Enslow Publishing, LLC
101 W. 23rd Street, Suite 240, New York, NY 10011

Library of Congress Cataloging-in-Publication Data

Names: Evans, John Fredric, author.
Title: Geno Auriemma / by John Fredric Evans. Description: New York : Enslow Publishing, 2020. | Series: Championship coaches | Includes bibliographical references and index. | Audience: Grade 7-12.
Identifiers: LCCN 2017055233| ISBN 9780766097919 (library bound) | ISBN 9780766097926 (pbk.)
Subjects: LCSH: Auriemma, Geno—Juvenile literature. | Basketball coaches—United States—Biography—Juvenile literature. | University of Connecticut—Basketball—Juvenile literature. | Connecticut Huskies (Basketball team)—Juvenile literature.
Classification: LCC GV884.A85 E83 2018 | DDC 796.323092 [B] —dc23
LC record available at https://lccn.loc.gov/2017055233

Printed in China

To Our Readers: We have done our best to make sure all website addresses in this book were active and appropriate when we went to press. However, the author and the publisher have no control over and assume no liability for the material available on those websites or on any websites they may link to. Any comments or suggestions can be sent by email to customerservice@enslow.com.

Photo Credits: Cover, pp. 1, 5, 16 Focus On Sport/Getty Images; p. 9 Tim Cammett/ WireImage/Getty Images; p. 13 Paul Fearn/Alamy Stock Photo; pp. 20, 24, 33, 47, 75, 91 © AP Images; p. 26 Ronald C. Modra/Sports Imagery/Getty Images; p. 30 Sporting News Archive/Getty Images; p. 34 Bettmann/Getty Images; p. 39 Kirby Lee/ Getty Images; p. 43 Al Bello/Getty Images; pp. 51, 87 Boston Globe/Getty Images; p. 55 Matt Campbell/AFP/Getty Images; p. 61 George Gojkovich/Getty Images; p. 66 Andy Lyons/Getty Images; p. 71 Nick Laham/Getty Images; p. 81 Jamie Squire/ Getty Images; p. 92 Maddie Meyer/Getty Images.

CONTENTS

INTRODUCTION

- - - - - - - - - - - - - - - -

Geno Auriemma holds the most Naismith College Coach of the Year Awards in the history of college basketball. An Italian immigrant who didn't even speak English when he came to the United States at age seven, Auriemma rose from the most modest of beginnings to build a dynasty at the University of Connecticut. He even shattered the records of famed men's coach John Wooden when UConn won its eleventh NCAA championship in 2016.

Driven by an insatiable need to succeed, Auriemma pushes star players harder than anyone. "I bother my best players," he said. "I poke and I prod and I push and I cajole and I irritate, because I want to find out, right from the opening day, how they are going to react under stress. They are going to have to handle the most stress of anyone on the team."[1]

"Geno wins because he makes the best players better versions of themselves,"[2] said Oklahoma Sooners coach Sherri Coale, whom he mentored when she was a high school coach.

"His real genius is his sense of people," former Huskies star Shea Ralph said. "He knows what motivates each one, what people can and can't do. When I played for him, he made me feel I had it in me to be better... I never thought I was capable of doing the things I did here."[3]

Auriemma was enshrined in the Naismith Basketball Hall of Fame in 2006. However, the winning streaks and NCAA championship trophies are just part of the picture. His program has changed the landscape of women's college basketball. Since UConn's 35–0 season in 1994–95, the popularity of the game has surged. In 2017, ESPN more than doubled its payment for WNBA broadcast rights, from $12 million to $25 million. In addition to packing their own arena every night, the Huskies attract record crowds on the road.

The growth of national television coverage and the formation of the WNBA can be attributed to the success of UConn and Tennessee, another boldface name in women's basketball. Like any great sports rivalry, the competing programs—and personalities—captured the

Geno Auriemma celebrates the United States' gold medal with two of his players, Diana Taurasi (*left*) and Sue Bird (*right*), at the 2016 Olympic Games in Rio. Taurasi and Bird also played for Auriemma at UConn.

imagination of the public. One indicator of the sport's growing popularity came when their televised 1995 clash garnered a front-page story in the *New York Times*. The paper has covered UConn ever since.

"When I look back, there were two primary developments in the 1990s that helped make the WNBA possible: the explosion of women's college basketball, and the 1996 Olympics in Atlanta," former WNBA commissioner Val Ackerman told the *Hartford Courant*. "There's no question that the early victories and championship by UConn helped put women's basketball on the map."[4]

Auriemma understood from the early stages of this phenomenon that the attention the Huskies were getting would increase interest in women's basketball at other schools. The more UConn won, and the more revenue their success generated, the more attention universities devoted to their own women's programs. "After a while, people got tired of getting their brains bashed in by Connecticut," said Auriemma. "It helped in recruiting. 'Why don't you come here and help us beat Connecticut's butt?'"[5]

If a team gave UConn a good test, even a moral victory inspired players and fans alike. This was big-time basketball, orchestrated by an outspoken "love him or hate him" personality.

Auriemma has a reputation for speaking the unvarnished truth to players and reporters alike, often in salty language. He colloquially refers to his players as "guys" and calls them "man," seeing these as generic terms. He is quick with a wisecrack. Carefully choosing his words is not a strength or a priority, whether the cameras are on or not. "I tell my players all the time, 'Your biggest strength is your biggest weakness.' The media loves to ask me questions. Why? Because they know I'm going to give them a straight answer. What's my biggest weakness? I give them a straight answer."[6]

And for all his bravado, Auriemma has no illusions about the secret to his success. "If Diana Taurasi had gone to another school, if Swin Cash or Rebecca Lobo or Jen Rizzotti or Sue Bird had gone somewhere else, who knows what would have happened to me? If Red Auerbach hadn't coached so many Hall of Famers, maybe he wouldn't be considered one of the greatest coaches who ever lived. It's the people you surround yourself with that dictate your success. If you are fortunate enough to surround yourself with the right people, then you reach a level of success that other people only dream about."[7]

The certainty with which he speaks has been seen as confident to the point of arrogance. However, Auriemma is often the first to admit that he is his own harshest critic. "You need a certain level of confidence to be successful at anything," he says. "I certainly have confidence. People think I have too much of it, and say it comes across as cocky, but the truth is, no matter what I accomplish, I'm never sure it's good enough."[8]

Auriemma is always striving for the perfect game, both from himself and every one of his players. If that is not accomplished—win or lose—he's haunted by what went wrong and the mistakes made. His success may stem from a unique combination of not giving a rip about what others think and caring about the game more than almost anyone.

1

FORGING A WORK ETHIC

Geno Auriemma was born in Montella, a small mountain village east of Naples, Italy, in 1954. His family had no car, television, or even a radio. Winters were very cold. Lacking electricity or heat, the Auriemmas would sleep in front of the fireplace. They heated water over an open flame. One morning when Geno was two, the winter cold was especially chilling. Geno fell asleep near a pile of hot coals used to keep sleeping babies warm and toppled over, belly first, onto the coals. His parents were at work, and the kids too young to work weren't watching.

Though Auriemma has no memory of the incident, the burn scars are a constant reminder of the conditions he grew up in and the advantages his family did not have. In the course of his life, he would come to see difficult experiences in a similar way. "Scars are part of you, whether you like it or not," said Auriemma. "Once you've been

Montella, the birthplace of Geno Auriemma, is a quaint village in Italy best known for its chestnuts.

scarred, the marks remain forever. The key is, what effect does it have on you going forward?"[1]

As difficult as it was for Geno in Montella, he didn't know what he was missing in the way of modern comforts. Nor did he understand what his parents had gone through, living in Italy during World War II. His mother, Marsiella, didn't attend school at any level. Though she never learned to read or write, she was a capable, resourceful person. She had to contend with the German occupation of Italy, which put her in life-or-death situations. After that, little intimidated her. "That's how I [first] got to see women as being tough," said Auriemma. "My vision as a coach is not about girls who can't do stuff. They're tough, they can do anything."[2]

Geno's father, Donato, was a very old world, masculine, blue-collar man. "In his mind, you measured success and hard work by how much physical labor you put into it,"[3] Auriemma said. Consequently, Donato never really understood why women's basketball meant so much for so many people or why his son's national championships were huge achievements.

Geno's father left to get a factory job in Norristown, Pennsylvania, and sent for his family in 1960. It took thirteen days for the boat to travel from Naples to Ellis Island. At seven years old, Geno arrived not knowing how to speak English, let alone how to act like an American. He wore home-made clothes to his second-grade class and brought different food to lunch than the other kids had seen. He certainly did not fit in right away.

The family moved in with Geno's uncle, where four adults and seven kids would share a three-bedroom house. Geno read everything he could get his hands on, even cereal boxes, and by the end of the school year he'd

Famed for Chestnuts and a Coach

Montella, Italy, is officially the sister city of Norristown, Pennsylvania, where the Auriemma family relocated when Geno was seven. While the area around Montella has been inhabited since the end of the Stone Age, the population remains around eight thousand. A picturesque community, Montella is flanked by mountains and cloaked in chestnut trees. The chestnuts produced there (*castagne*, in Italian) are world famous. In fact, Montella hosts an annual chestnut festival and has a museum dedicated to them.

mastered the language well
enough to be promoted to
third grade. His parents didn't
have credit cards or a checking
account, so he would pay their
bills in person, with cash,

> "He's still the responsible first child who wants to make sure everybody is all right."[4]
>
> — Kathy Auriemma

because he could communicate with the people at the bank, electric
company, and corner market.

THE COURT CALLED TO HIM

Fortunately, two boys took Geno under their wing and made sure
no one bullied him for being different. They also gave him his first
true introduction to sports. Because they could play right there in
the neighborhood, the boys focused on baseball. Geno took to it
immediately. At age thirteen, he played little league for coach Vern
Schlotzhauer, whom he would never forget.

Though Geno was one of the best players on the team, Vern named
another boy most valuable player. The coach knew that winning this
award meant a lot to Geno, and continuing to strive for it would
bring out the best in him. Geno applied the same motivational tech-
nique with his own players years later. He came to believe that athletes won't reach their fullest potential if their coach doesn't make
them prove themselves, again and again.

In ninth grade, Geno tried out for the Bishop Kenrick High School
team but didn't make the cut. Motivated by this failure, he began

playing every afternoon. The next year he tried out again and became the team's backup point guard. Even as a "bench-warmer," Geno was happy to be a member of the team and admired his coach, Buddy Gardler, greatly. Gardler had a plainspoken, no-nonsense coaching style. Sound familiar?

COLLEGE-BOUND

In college, Auriemma learned another lesson that would linger with him. Back then he couldn't be bothered with classes that didn't capture his interest. Consequently, he can relate to players tempted to cut class or skip study sessions. He understands how easy it can be to miss the big picture. For college athletes, not making your grades can cost you a scholarship and, potentially, your athletic career. "I make sure our kids take their academics very seriously," said Auriemma. "Part of that is probably because I didn't do that when I was young. I got by. I didn't bother to excel, and I regret it. I don't want any of my players to look back and say, 'I should have studied more. I should have gotten more out of my classes.'"[5]

He met his future wife, Kathy, when they were freshmen at Montgomery Community College in Blue Bell, Pennsylvania. He played hoops, and she was a cheerleader. She has said their roles haven't changed that much since then. "To be honest, I was smitten with him the first time I saw him," said Kathy. "We were a lot alike."[6]

Kathy is as much a part of the program "family" as he is. She's been known to visit the locker room after a win and dance with players.

"She cares about you," said Rebecca Lobo. "She's not just a 'yes man,' she provides balance to [Geno] and there is no b.s. when you talk to her. She is no shrinking violet and she is a woman who can listen to your problems, set you straight..."[7]

Auriemma's first coaching job was as an assistant at St. Joseph's University in Philadelphia, where he worked in 1978 and 1979. To keep the bills paid he had to moonlight in the steel mills, pour drinks, teach gym classes, and stock shelves in a grocery store. The steel mill was the worst. He wore a water-saturated bandanna over his face to screen out the sulfur fumes.

After working as an assistant at his old high school for a couple of years, Auriemma's big break came when he was hired by Debbie

In addition to being his most trusted confidante, Geno's wife, Kathy, is a pillar of the program. Many players see her as a second mom.

Geno's Mentor and Champion

Though she was just two years older than Auriemma, Debbie Ryan had already been the women's basketball coach at the University of Virginia for four years when she hired him. She would hold the job for thirty years, winning almost 70 percent of the 1,059 games she coached. In 2001, Ryan coached the US basketball team to a gold medal at the World University Games in Beijing. A fierce competitor on and off the court, Ryan led Virginia to twenty-four NCAA Tournament appearances (reaching the championship game in 1991) and overcame a pancreatic cancer diagnosis in 2000.

Ryan, coach of the University of Virginia Cavaliers. Virginia was a top 20 women's basketball program.

In his first two years with Virginia, Auriemma recruited six high school all-Americans. In his third year the Cavaliers went 24–8 and won the ACC regular season title.

Coaching at Virginia for four years, Auriemma learned a lot from Debbie Ryan, but he played a very different role than he would as a head coach. His role as an assistant was more "good cop" to Ryan's "bad cop," as he sympathized with the players and interpreted Ryan's instructions for them. Still, Auriemma knew that it would need to be different when he was in charge of his own program. He saw how Ryan's players responded to her hard coaching, and he knew that would motivate him, if he was in their shoes.

One thing was certain—
Auriemma was ready to take
the next step in his career.
Ryan described him, even at
that age, as "a supremely confident human being."[9]

> "You're either a risk taker or
> you're not, and if you don't take
> risks, you'll never win big."[8]
> — Geno Auriemma

The opportunity to do it his way came in 1985, when Auriemma received a phone call from Storrs, Connecticut. He was invited to interview for the vacant head coaching position with the University of Connecticut's women's basketball team.

2

NO WARM WELCOME IN STORRS

- - - - - - - - - - - - - - - -

Years later, it was revealed that originally the search committee at Connecticut wanted to hire a woman. "I was committed to hiring the best woman for the position," said associate director of athletics Pat Meiser-McKnett. "If there were two candidates who graded out the same and one was male and the other female, we were clearly going to take the female."[1]

Still, Debbie Ryan recommended Auriemma, giving him an edge. He was the aggressive, hard-charging presence the search committee wanted. And he wasn't as demanding as other candidates. "In my (UConn) interview I said, 'Listen, don't worry about giving me anything. This is not going to be as hard as you think. Just give me three

Auriemma's aggressive attitude and brash confidence got him the job with UConn.

or four years and we'll be in the Top 25.' They said, 'What?' I said, 'Yeah, it's only going to take me three or four years and we'll be in the Top 25.' [Heck] no, I didn't believe any of it."[2]

Though the Huskies played in the Big East, a legitimate conference growing stronger every year, Auriemma knew this was a small-time program in a sport few schools were fully committed to supporting at the time. He was offered the job over coffee at Dunkin' Donuts.

"I don't hire good coaches, I hire good people. If they turn out to be good coaches, too, that's a plus."[3]

— Geno Auriemma

JUST THE BEGINNING

Auriemma saw the job as a stepping-stone, a place to build a reputation before moving on. "I saw the negatives," said Auriemma. "I thought I would try to overcome them for as long as I could… I wasn't going to kill myself if there weren't going to be changes. I would go someplace else to win a national championship."[4]

Immediately after signing a five-year contract, Auriemma made a critical hire of his own. Chris Dailey, twenty-six, was a top assistant at Rutgers, where she had played college ball. Auriemma believed that hiring the person in charge of recruiting is a new coach's most important decision. While at Virginia, Auriemma recruited against Dailey. He knew she was a great judge of both talent and character. He told Dailey that at UConn she would have the chance to build a program from the ground up.

Dailey was Auriemma's first and most valuable recruit. As he did the public relations, she pounded the pavement, finding talented kids and coordinating their recruiting.

Auriemma and Dailey would share an office the size of a walk-in closet. Their administrative assistant divided her time with seventeen other sports programs. Dailey and the men's track coach shared a phone line. For recruiting visits, the university motor pool issued them a subcompact car, a less-than-stylish 1982 Chevy Chevette.

Auriemma's players shared a small and shabby locker room with the softball team. The school's dilapidated field house had a leaky roof, so when it rained they had to place buckets around the basketball court. Meanwhile, members of the track team and baseball players also used the building. Though a large curtain was drawn around the court, there were distractions aplenty. Sometimes an errant baseball would whiz past players' heads or a starter's pistol would go off nearby. Weight lifters blasted music so loud that Auriemma had to shout his instructions to his players. Needless to say, conditions were less than ideal.

In Need of a Leader

Originally, women's basketball at UConn was little more than an intramural program that played in occasional intercollegiate competitions. In 1974, the university shifted the team from the physical education department to the department of athletics, beginning the modern era of women's hoops at UConn. In its first eleven years, the team posted a single winning season, a 16–14 campaign in 1980–81. The team then managed a 36–74 record before the arrival of Geno Auriemma.

That first year, Auriemma was working with his predecessor's players. He thought that only one of them truly belonged at the Division I level, where they'd be competing. With a roster lacking talent, Auriemma focused on getting the fundamentals down. In practice, they ran drill after drill after drill. This got the players in great shape, if nothing else.

Around fifty fans showed up for UConn women's games, which were free. Sporadically a newspaper writer would attend, seldom with a photographer. It was a struggle to get the score of a game included in the small print of the newspaper's agate page. All this would soon

change, however. Within a few years, the home crowd would regu-
larly reach ten thousand.

Auriemma's first season was his only losing season. The team finished
12–15 with four Big East wins, including three in a row. It was the first
time UConn had won that many division games. The season also featured the first seven-game winning streak in school history. "I don't
think I've ever had a team work harder than that first team," Auriemma
said. "That's still my favorite team of all time to coach. They were lousy,
but they didn't know it. What I learned from that first year is that if you
give kids some hope, they will respond. I don't think I have ever had a
team respond better to what I tried to do than that team."[5]

Chris Dailey is Auriemma's trusted, long-standing assistant coach. She
helped him turn a losing program into one that draws in top recruits.

"Even when we were bad, we played hard," said Dailey. "That has always been our trademark. The difference now is that we are playing hard with better players."[6]

LAMB WAS A LION

Going into Geno's second season, his top recruit was Kris Lamb, a five-foot-eleven guard from Virginia and a high school all-American. Lamb was the first key recruit to take a chance on a program that wasn't well established. The fact that she came all the way from Virginia was a statement of confidence in Auriemma—she met him at a basketball camp he helped run as an assistant coach. Demonstrating how to create space when going up for a rebound, Auriemma accidently elbowed Lamb in the nose. She barely flinched, and Auriemma knew he was dealing with a tough player.

Though Lamb became a part of Auriemma's family immediately, coming over for dinner and even babysitting his kids, her relationship with Auriemma didn't mean he took it easy on her. Knowing what drove Lamb made him coach her all the harder. "It's like when you raise a bunch of kids," Auriemma said. "Do you really think you're harder on your last kid than you are on your first or second kid? Of course not, not in a million years."[7]

One day the Huskies had a huge lead on Pittsburgh, and Lamb headed to the bench with only one field goal on twelve attempts. When Auriemma saw that she was crying, he stormed up to her and said, "You've got to be kidding me. We're up fifteen and you're sitting here crying because you're not shooting well. This is so much about you it's unbelievable."[8] Lamb was speechless, but she learned a lesson every star player would, in her time in Storrs: care about the team's performance, not your own stats. Lamb became the heart and soul of the Huskies as the team went 14–13.

The following year, Auriemma and Chris Dailey's recruiting took a big step forward with the addition of Kerry Bascom and Laura Lishness, the most highly regarded signees in school history. Bascom thrived within the give-and-take of Auriemma's challenging coaching style.

On paper, this looked like a talented bunch, one that could make some noise in the Big East. But chemistry problems arose within the team, which finished 17–11. "There was a sense on that team that it was made up of some of my guys and some of the other coach's people," said Auriemma. "The new guys wanted to show that they had ridden in on white horses and were going to build the program, while the older guys were thinking, 'what are we, chopped liver? He must not have any confidence

The Carolina Way

Geno Auriemma has expressed great admiration for Dean Smith's North Carolina Tar Heels, calling Smith one of the most influential coaches of all time. In 1967, Smith was among the first coaches in the segregated South to offer a scholarship to a black athlete. More than 96 percent of his players graduated. The now-familiar "point to the passer," by which a scorer acknowledges a teammate's assist, originated in the team-first "Carolina Way." As an assistant at Virginia, Auriemma listened to Smith's pregame and halftime speeches whenever North Carolina played the men's team.

in us because he is bringing in all these new people.'"[9]

The divide between Auriemma's recruits and the players he inherited created a "turf war" of sorts. Auriemma

> "I demand sometimes more than they can give. But I don't know what that is until I find out."[10]
>
> — Geno Auriemma

tried to bring them together but failed. He thought the team could have won twenty games, but key intangibles were missing. Worse, the old guard tried to get Auriemma and Dailey fired after the season. They brought up an incident that occurred during a bad loss to Hartford, a team they should have beaten. Delivering an impassioned halftime speech, Auriemma saw Kris Lamb sitting with her head in her hands.

He later recounted the incident in his autobiography. "I go over to her, and I whack her arms off her knees and I tell her, 'You look me in the eye when I'm talking to you. Do you understand?' She's a little startled, but mostly she's ticked off, so she stares at me with complete disdain, and I rant a little more, and then we go out and win the game by twenty-three points."[11]

When Auriemma's boss asked him about it, he said that he wouldn't have done that with any other player, but Lamb was like a daughter to him and he knew she understood the point he was making. Though Lamb and her family stuck up for Auriemma, rumors swirled around the state that he had punched her. It was a difficult time, but it taught Auriemma that some lines simply should not be crossed.

3

CHEMISTRY TESTS

- - - - - - - - - - - - - - - -

With most of the unhappy players moving on—there would be no seniors on the squad—another infusion of new blood changed the team's makeup in 1988–89. The roster featured two sophomores, three juniors, and six freshman. Newcomers Debbie Baer, Meghan Pattyson, Wendy Davis, and Stacey Wetzel represented a turning point in the development of the program. "That class put us over the top," Dailey said. "It gave us numbers and versatility. It also gave us the type of kid, the type of work ethic, that would define Connecticut basketball."[1]

HE'S GOT PERSONALITY

Dailey has always known what kind of player will be a good fit with Geno Auriemma. To this day, a compatible personality is more important than a player's ability. Early on, the people at UConn were more of a calling card than the school's facilities. To choose UConn, a player had to really want to play for Auriemma and compete alongside her new teammates.

The 1988–89 season was one of transformation and unprecedented success. Becoming a unified, well-synchronized basketball machine, the Huskies won both the Big East regular season and tournament titles, earned a national ranking (29th), and received the school's first-ever invite to the NCAA Tournament. Though the Huskies lost to La Salle in the first round, 72–63, people were paying attention.

Meghan Pattyson thrived under Auriemma's tough coaching.

Crowds grew throughout the season as this young team proved itself. Bascom was named Big East Player of the Year, and Auriemma won the conference's Coach of the Year Award.

In 1989–90 the team earned their first Top 25 national ranking and set new attendance records. One of sixteen seeded teams entering the then-forty-eight-team NCAA Tournament, UConn lost to Clemson 61–59 in the second round.

> *"With the absence of pressure, it's hard to do great things."*[2]
>
> — Geno Auriemma

Looking back on this early exit from the tournament, Auriemma felt he took things for granted entering the Clemson game. "I don't need to harp on that again. I don't need to keep an eye on certain things like I used to," he remembered thinking. "So I let things go, and we won twenty-five games. But we weren't as good. The telling thing was at the end of that year. Meghan Pattyson comes to me—we're having year-end wrap-ups—and I say to her, 'what do you think, Meg?' And she says to me, 'I think you were a bit of a wuss this year. I think you need to get back to where you were. I don't think you were hard enough on us.'"[3]

Entering 1990–91, the Huskies became the first Big East team to be nationally ranked in the preseason. They began playing in a new, modern facility, the Harry A. Gampel Pavilion, which accommodated ten thousand fans. Its dome resembled Epcot Center, and what went on beneath it was just as entertaining. The Huskies hit their stride that year.

On the first day of practice, Auriemma told the team that their goal was a Final Four appearance. He had scheduled a forbidding out-of-conference slate featuring upper-echelon teams. Though UConn lost a couple of those games,

Family First

Over the years Auriemma has lost out on his share of recruits, perhaps none more talented than Elena Delle Donne. The "do it all" kind of player that Auriemma covets, Delle Donne accepted a UConn scholarship but left the program after just two days. She wasn't ready to be separated from her family, especially her older sister Lizzie, who suffers from cerebral palsy and is both blind and deaf. Ultimately, Delle Donne played hoops at Delaware before being taken No. 2 overall by the WNBA's Chicago Sky. She was voted league MVP in 2015.

Auriemma often lands the recruits he wants, but Elena Delle Donne declined her scholarship to be closer to a family member who needed her.

playing a high level of competition honed the Huskies' game. Any doubts about their potential were dispelled in early December when UConn edged No. 2–ranked Auburn 67–63 in the program's biggest victory to date.

From there, UConn tore off fourteen wins in a row and ended the regular season with a No. 13 national ranking. Their final mark was 23–4, and they won their third Big East title in a row. By now Huskies tickets

> *"As a person he is very funny and has a great personality."*[4]
>
> — **Rebecca Lobo**

were no longer free, and New England Sports Network televised five of their games. But did the team reach their preseason goal? In the NCAA Tournament, Auriemma remembers coaching like a "lunatic" because he sensed the team was close to a breakthrough.

After Auriemma was a "wild man on the sidelines" in a win over Clemson, the team made the Final Four. In an interesting twist of fate, they'd be playing Auriemma's old team. Virginia was ranked No. 1 at one point during the season and posed a stiff challenge. The officiating became a factor when Kerry Bascom picked up two questionable fouls and spent vital minutes on the bench. Laura Lishness had a subpar game. Despite their top seniors struggling, the team still found itself down only two points with seventeen seconds on the clock. It wasn't meant to be, though—Virginia hit foul shots to pull away and win 61–55.

After the game, Auriemma believed they would have beaten Tennessee in the final, had they only gotten past the Cavaliers. "Tennessee was big and slow and would not have been able to guard our perimeter people," he said. "We could have won the national championship that year."[5]

As is customary for the coach, Auriemma put most of the blame on himself. "I let them proceed at their own pace, just like I had done the year earlier, and it caught up to us. I didn't have them on the edge. I had spent the whole year [ticking] them off at the right moment and now, for that particular game, I let them cruise."[6]

Feeling burned, Auriemma resolved to maintain his relentless intensity in the future.

A WOLF WOULD LEAD THE PACK

The 1991–92 season would not include Bascom and Lishness, who graduated. Auriemma and Dailey found more than adequate reinforcements, however. Arriving that year were new recruits Pam Webber and

Rebecca Lobo. Lobo was a huge get for the up-and-coming UConn program. After setting a new Massachusetts state scoring record, she was recruited by more than a hundred colleges. "She was the first nationally known player we were fortunate enough to get," Auriemma said. "Next thing you know, everybody in America is talking about the University of Connecticut women and Rebecca Lobo."[7]

Lobo came to UConn to play for Auriemma and Dailey. "Obviously, he was a good coach," she said of Auriemma. "I could tell that by his record and the way practice went. As a person he is very funny and has a great personality. And that is what I was looking for in a coach, off the court. Someone who I could go in and see them in their office and sit down and talk. The people are what drove me.

As seen in this 2010 Final Four matchup with Baylor, Auriemma's demeanor during games can be fiery. His teams feed off that intensity.

They could have had a losing record, and I probably still would have come here just because I felt so good about the people."[8]

That focus on who someone is as a person was mutual. Auriemma has always put a premium on how a recruit would fit into the team fabric. "In recruiting, a 'five' is a superstar, a Rebecca Lobo coming out of high school," Auriemma said. "I would take a kid who is a four, if I thought she had all the intangibles it takes for winning, over a kid who is a five but is missing those things. I think in the long run we win more games because of it."[9]

Auriemma still had the Baer-Davis-Pattyson class, selfless players with lots of big-game experience, but the changing of the guard would take time. His new-look team lost in the second round of the NCAAs. The 1992–93 edition was ousted in the first round of the tournament. In two years, the program had graduated all five of its starters, which made it tough to compete with the nation's best teams. Still, the nucleus of a championship roster was quietly forming. Sophomores Lobo and Webber were already the team's best players, and gifted freshmen Jen Rizzotti and Jamelle Elliott were fiercely competitive. With another year of growth and seasoning, this would be a strong team.

One year later, the 1993–94 team had the firepower to go far. Every season has its pivot points where things could go either way. One such moment came when Auriemma pulled his starters at the twelve-minute mark of a loss to Seton Hall. On that day he wanted to lose by as many points as possible, and the margin ballooned to twenty by the final buzzer. He thought the group "looked tired" and "had no life." They needed a jolt of fresh inspiration.

Sitting and watching their opponents celebrate and win had the desired effect on his star players. The Huskies finished conference play with a 17–1 record and went 30–3 overall. In the NCAA Tournament, UConn played their way into the Elite Eight. There, they faced a North Carolina team that Auriemma has said was too strong and too fast for them, that day. The defeat was historically significant—it was the last game they would lose for more than a year.

Heart of the Huskies

Over the years, the counsel of Auriemma's wife, Kathy, has benefited both Auriemma and the team, whom she calls her "extra daughters." She has always been there for players in need of a mother's advice, miles from their own. "I think I'm whatever they need me to be," said Kathy of her role in their lives. "When you think of the brains of UConn basketball, you think of Coach Auriemma," said former player Stefanie Dolson. "But when you think of the heart, you think of Mrs. A."[10]

The summer before the 1994–95 season, the team went to Europe to play top European teams. Dailey and Auriemma instituted a new offense, one made famous by Michael Jordan's NBA champion Chicago Bulls. The triangle offense relies on unselfishness, as it requires that players pass often and make sharp cuts in order to open an area for their teammates, fully knowing someone else will get the glory. Well executed, the offense resembles a choreographed dance that is beautiful to watch. Auriemma's players picked it up quickly and were soon running the triangle to perfection.

Auriemma described UConn's offense as "The creative movement of five people, flowing, like a musician creating rhythm with his music. In an ideal world, this is what basketball is all about, movement that can't be scouted by the opposition."[11] Something special was happening here.

4

THE PURSUIT
OF PERFECTION

I t came as no surprise that the men's and women's basketball teams at UConn were good in 1994–95, but together they would exceed their fans' wildest expectations. Auriemma's squad returned every key player from the year before and added Nykesha Sales, a big, athletic guard who would ultimately break the school scoring record (in controversial fashion).

That year no other top contender for the NCAA championship had come out ahead after all their seniors graduated. Still, to Auriemma success was not measured in wins, which he knew would come. He wanted winning to be the natural result of playing extremely well. "We never talked about winning," said Auriemma. "Playing at a certain level was our goal. And whenever we didn't reach that level, everyone was [ticked]."[1]

Those Huskies routinely beat teams by 35 points, but it might have been 50 if their starters played more than twenty-five minutes a game. The criteria to measure the team's performance was a series of goals for each game, goals that meant little individually but everything when taken collectively. "The little goals became our barometer because they are all the things that lead to winning," Auriemma said. "We'd have this sheet up there with twelve goals. The ones we hit would get highlighted. If we only got six, that means in six other areas in which we tried to be good, we were lousy, regardless of the score."[2]

> *"Chemistry is the ingredient present in most great teams."*[3]
>
> — Geno Auriemma

IT'S THE DESTINATION AND THE JOURNEY

Auriemma was determined to reap the rewards of the painful lesson learned when he eased up on the team at the wrong time and they lost their edge. This year he stayed on them all the time, maintaining their standards of excellence, but he did it "the right way" and the kids were the "right kids," so they enjoyed the journey. The chemistry experiment that was the 1994–95 Huskies did not blow up in Auriemma's face. This time it was a perfect formula for success.

"Chemistry is the ingredient present in most great teams," said Auriemma. "People who have chemistry are people who take the time to listen to what you have to say. They're not into themselves, their egos are intact, they are a giving, sacrificing type of person.

That is the kind of person who will pass you the ball when you are wide open. Kids that are unselfish to begin with are going to play unselfishly."[4]

This has remained true with each incarnation of the team. "The way Connecticut's run… there's no time for [egos]," said Sue Bird, who joined the program in 1998. "He was so demanding, had such high expectations, that there's nothing better than doing it right. That's the biggest 'take that!' ever. And he loves that. He wants you to have that. Something he always drilled into us was if he's being hard on you and if you can continually make the plays, that's the

In her final game, powerhouse Nykesha Sales broke UConn's scoring record at the time.

best thing for your confidence. You know you're a big-time player if you can do that."[5]

In 1994–95, Auriemma was grateful for players like Pam Webber, who never missed a practice or even a workout; Wendy Davis, a straight-A student who brought that same work ethic to the court; Jen Rizzotti, who once mopped a wet spot on the floor when the game officials didn't; and Rebecca Lobo, always first off the bench to greet a teammate coming off the court.

UConn faced the last team to beat them, Seton Hall, in January 1995. The media billed it as a serious challenge to the 12–0 Huskies, as Seton Hall was ranked No. 19 in the nation. UConn won 80–26. They faced Tennessee three days later before a national audience on ESPN. Pat Summitt's Lady Volunteers were 16–0 and had a dozen high school all-Americans. Tennessee was ranked No. 1 and UConn No. 2. In contrast to the early days, when photographers were rarely seen at UConn games, there were 156 members of the media courtside. The team had already sold out their last six games of the season—a far cry from fifty fans showing up to watch the home team.

Before an exuberant sellout crowd at Gampel Pavilion, the Huskies took a 41–33 lead into the locker room at halftime. Tennessee made a run and Auriemma called time out, up five with nine minutes to play. Lobo took over the next five minutes, playing like a woman

An Unlikely Achievement

On the morning of February 14, 1995, the UConn men joined the women's team at the top, marking the first time in NCAA history that men's and women's teams from the same university held the No. 1 designation at the same time. The women were elevated after a victory over then-top-ranked Tennessee at Gampel Pavilion. In this poll the 19–0 women garnered thirty-two of thirty-three first-place votes. According to a professor of information studies at Syracuse, the chances of a school's basketball teams combining to achieve this feat was one in 88,486. [6]

The 1995 Huskies completed an undefeated season with a 70–64 win over Tennessee to win the NCAA title.

possessed. Then Kara Wolters, Elliott, and Rizzotti made baskets and free throws to clinch a 77–66 win. Auriemma watched his giddy players form a pile-up on the floor as the fans gave them a standing ovation. "This is one of the toughest places we've played," said Summitt. "That kind of atmosphere and support give them a sixth-player effect."[7]

"I'll wake up tomorrow with a smile on my face," Lobo said after the win. "But in practice tomorrow I'll go back to being the worst post player in the country."[8] She was joking, but there is truth in jest—her coach wouldn't ease up on his players now that true greatness lay within in their grasp.

HUSKY MANIA

That season the UConn women mowed down the opposition by an average of 35 points per game, finishing the regular season 26–0. They breezed through the Big East Tournament and entered the NCAA as a No. 1 seed. Their first test came in the East Regional Final, where they faced Debbie Ryan's Virginia Cavaliers once again. Playing his old boss and friend was always special for Auriemma, but this was also an Elite Eight game and the last contest in Gampel Pavilion for Lobo and Webber. At stake were the Huskies' unbeaten record and a berth in the Final Four.

Auriemma remembers everyone being jittery in the first half, including himself. UConn got out to an early lead but frittered it away to trail 44–37 at half. Amazingly, it was the team's first halftime deficit of the year. The game got very physical in the second half, which

> *"It's about doing it in a way that it can't be done any better."*[9]
>
> — Geno Auriemma

favored the Huskies. With 4:39 left in the game they pulled in front, 66–57. Virginia then cut the lead to 66–63. The last two minutes were a defensive struggle, and Lobo blocked a last-minute three-point attempt to seal the victory.

UConn then traveled to Minneapolis to face the always-deep, always-dangerous Stanford Cardinal in the Final Four. Though Stanford had twelve all-Americans, UConn entered the game a seven-point favorite. Kara Wolters could not be guarded that day, scoring 31 of the team's 69 front-court points, to just 19 for Stanford's "bigs." The Huskies held Stanford star Kate Starbird to two points in twenty-six minutes. UConn's 87–60 win set a new record for largest margin of victory in the fourteen-year history of the women's Final Four.

To the surprise of no one, Tennessee awaited them in the national championship game. Summitt had the Lady Vols ready to end this rematch with a different outcome, and most experts agreed with her. Tennessee was still considered the better team, and they were playing better than in January. "I'm not sure anyone can beat Tennessee twice in the same season," Auriemma said in his postgame press conference after the Stanford win. "I don't think Geno believes that," Summit responded, when this was relayed to her. "But I hope he's right."[10]

Auriemma wasn't telling the cameras one thing and his players another. He kept the team focused by convincing them they would lose by double digits if they didn't match the Vols' intensity. "We just have to be tougher than them because they fancy themselves the toughest, strongest, most intense, mentally tough team in America," Auriemma warned his players. "They are not going to fall apart in the championship game."[11]

At tipoff, viewership in Connecticut surpassed even the 1995 Super Bowl. Two of every three TV sets in use were tuned to the women's basketball game. More people watched than had ever watched a college hoops game in the state.[12]

This confrontation lived up to the hype. Auriemma was dismayed to see Lobo, Wolters, and Rizzotti in foul trouble for most of the first

Auriemma (Coach of the Year) and Rebecca Lobo (National Player of the Year) hold the hardware they won for their fantastic 1994-95 season.

half. He was reminded of Kerry Bascom's similar problems in the 1991 Final Four, tripping up a team two wins away from a national championship. Still, the Vols struggled to build a six-point lead at halftime.

In the locker room, Auriemma noted that his team had a considerable edge on the glass, grabbing a dozen rebounds to Tennessee's three. Rebounds give your team extra shots and deny the other team those opportunities. "If we outrebound them in the second half, we win the game," he told the Huskies.

Tennessee pushed the lead to nine early in the second half, but UConn showed grit and determination. Down six with 11:32 to play, Lobo hit four of five shots as UConn closed the gap to 58–55.

A Rizzotti layup gave UConn the lead with less than two minutes to go. Lobo came down with two critical rebounds and made three free throws down the stretch as UConn emerged with a 70–64 win. They ended the game with ten more rebounds than Tennessee.

Finishing 35–0, UConn joined the 1986 Texas women as their sport's only programs to make it through an entire season without suffering a single loss. "We didn't set out to be perfect, but when they talk about Connecticut basketball in 1995, they are going to say we were perfect,"[14] said Auriemma after winning his first national championship. Among many other accolades, he won AP and Naismith Coach of the Year honors.

Lobo Leads the Way

After graduating, Rebecca Lobo increased the visibility of the women's game by starring on the US national team, which won gold at the 1996 Summer Olympics in Atlanta. She was one of the first three players signed to the WNBA when it launched in 1997. In 2017, Lobo was inducted into the Basketball Hall of Fame. "My senior year at UConn was one of the most magical seasons in the history of women's college basketball,"[13] she said in her acceptance speech, before thanking Auriemma and her teammates by name.

5

GROWTH SPURTS

Returning home from Minneapolis, Auriemma was quiet and pensive even after being greeted by adoring crowds. "I think I was suffering from what women suffer right after they give birth, postpartum depression," he said. "It hit me right away. I was just so tired. All the stuff that we had held in, all this focus, this idea of every day thinking, 'be good today,' 'be good today,' never giving yourself a chance to look ahead or look behind… I just didn't have anything left."[1]

Lobo went on David Letterman's late-night talk show, solidifying her celebrity status. A month later one hundred thousand people turned out for a victory parade in Hartford, Connecticut. For only the third time in history a separate *Sports Illustrated* cover was issued for the Northeast region, featuring an action photo of Jen Rizzotti. The sixty-six thousand magazines sold out as soon as they hit the

After the 1995 NCAA win, the Huskies captured the attention of the nation. They met President Bill Clinton twice.

"Usually, smart people don't go into coaching."[2]

— **Geno Auriemma**

stands. Another forty-five thousand copies were printed and quickly snapped up.

Watching tape of the title game with his players, Auriemma paused it after five plays to point out a mistake someone made. Rizzotti turned around and threw something at him. But that was Auriemma, and she loved him for it. He was always seeing what wasn't perfect, what needed to be worked on. "Vince Lombardi said the difference between a good coach and a great coach is that a great coach knows when it looks right," Auriemma said. "Some guys never know what it's supposed to look like."[3]

CH-CH-CHANGES

Without Lobo the team wasn't the same, though Kara Wolters returned and Nykesha Sales was now a promising sophomore. The defending champions remained the best team in the country for much of the year as UConn went 34–4, 17–1 in conference, and made it to the Final Four again. This time Tennessee prevailed, however, as the Lady Vols pulled out an 88–83 win in a thrilling back-and-forth overtime game that fans still speak about in both Storrs and Knoxville.

The following year a high school legend, Shea Ralph, was an object of desire for many big-time schools. Auriemma talked to her on the phone one day, and she asked, "Coach, what kind of a role do you see for me if I come to UConn?" Auriemma responded, "Shea, I don't know. If you are really, really good, then you'll have a chance to play a lot. But if you suck, you won't play at all."[4]

As with much about Geno Auriemma, it was a "love it or hate it" statement that went a long way toward identifying whether or not a recruit was his kind of player or not. Shea Ralph was, and that's why she chose UConn.

With Ralph joining Wolters and Sales, the Huskies rolled through the regular season undefeated. They were dismayed when the year ended the same way 1995–96 had, though this time Tennessee ousted

Siberian Husky

Svetlana "Sveta" Abrosimova was the program's first three-time all-American and the seventh overall selection in the 2001 WNBA draft. Not just a spectacular scorer, she also finished her UConn career fifth in total steals, fifth in three-point shooting percentage, thirteenth in assists, and fourteenth in rebounds. Auriemma loved her dry wit even as her free-wheeling style of play drove him crazy at times. At one practice the Russian laughed when he threatened to send her back to Siberia for firing a no-look pass into the stands— Sveta had actually played for a club team in Siberia.

Connecticut in the Elite Eight, not the Final Four. Summitt and the Lady Vols went on to be crowned NCAA champions both times.

Worse than the losses was the fact that Shea Ralph tore her ACL in the tournament and then again in an August shoot-around, practically the first time she stepped back on the court. This raised a red flag for Auriemma, and it was discovered that Ralph had an eating disorder dating back to high school. Living on less than 1,000 calories a day, she wasn't providing her body with nearly enough energy to be healthy, let alone play her high-energy brand of college basketball. Ralph later admitted that while she didn't realize it at the time, anorexia probably hindered her recovery from the first knee injury. Auriemma and the team helped Ralph maintain a healthier diet from that point on.

Though Ralph missed the 1997–98 season, the team still compiled a 34–3 record. In an Elite Eight loss to North Carolina State, the short-handed Huskies were also without Sales. Meanwhile, the Lady Vols won their third straight championship in 1997–98, completing an undefeated season of their own.

TALENT, AND TROUBLE

Entering the 1998–99 season, UConn boasted a recruiting class that had every bit as much potential as the loaded Tennessee teams that were winning championships. Auriemma welcomed into the fold five high school stars: Tamika Williams, Asjha Jones, Swin Cash, Sue Bird, and Keirsten Walters. Exuberant fans called the freshmen "the TASSK Force," using the first initials from the players' first names.

Still in Storrs were Shea Ralph, now healthy, and Svetlana Abrosimova, better known as "Sveta," who'd come from Russia to score bushels of points for UConn.

And that she did. In the third game of the season, a win over UCLA, Sveta scored 39 points on just seventeen shots. UConn scored

> *"I feel like I failed them."*[5]
> — Geno Auriemma

113 points, the kind of number generally seen in the NBA. They would break the century mark in nine of their first thirteen games, winning all of them. Just ten games into the season, however, Sue Bird tore her ACL and was out for the year.

On occasion, Auriemma has had a hard time getting through to his team. He wants players to take practice as seriously as they treat games.

There were other problems holding them back. Auriemma struggled to teach his new players the fundamentals that other teams had seemed to grasp immediately. On one particularly frustrating occasion, he left a practice for the dark solitude to be found under the bleachers. Auriemma refused to come out until everyone had gone home for the day. His players wondered if their coach had suffered a nervous breakdown.

Auriemma was baffled to see so much talent yield so little tangible result. "During that 1998–99 season, for the first time this innate ability I've always had, to reach kids and get the absolute most of them, failed me," he said. "And I feel like I failed them."[6]

Class of the League

UConn's 1998–1999 freshman foursome of Sue Bird, Swin Cash, Asjha Jones, and Tamika Williams would earn countless college honors and go on to become first-round WNBA draft picks. Perhaps the greatest point guard in her sport's history, Bird (drafted first overall) has won two WNBA championships and four Olympic gold medals. The very competitive Cash won Olympic gold and led Detroit to its first WNBA title. Jones won gold with Auriemma at the 2012 Summer Olympics. Williams's career field-goal accuracy, 70.3 percent, is an NCAA record and she set a single-season mark (66.8 percent) in the WNBA.

The team was talented but rudderless. With so many underclassmen and Ralph coming off a season lost to injury, no one seemed ready to seize a leadership role. In the NCAA Tournament they almost lost to an eight-seed before going down in the Midwest

Regional Final to finish the season with a 29–5 record. By that point, losing five games felt like a letdown for everyone: Auriemma, the players, the school, and the state. As disappointed as he was, Auriemma knew that most kids need time to mature as a person before they can reach their potential as players. He was sure this group could be special, given that time to develop.

A photo was taken of Swin Cash crying on the bench, moments after the team's season-ending loss. Entering the next season, Auriemma noticed the photo taped up in her locker. "I don't want to ever forget what that felt like,"[7] she told Auriemma.

Looking back at these injury-marred seasons, Auriemma couldn't help but wonder what might have been. "It's easy to look back at the seasons and say, 'If this, if that. The only time we lost full-strength in the Final Four was 1996. And then in 1997 we had the best team in the country, by far. By far. And then Shea goes down and we didn't handle it well. Then in 1998, Kesha goes down. Then 1999, Sue goes down."[8]

6

THE RESURRECTION

Auriemma set out on the 1999–2000 campaign with mostly the same players as the year before. After a solid win in the opener, the team struggled in its first few minutes versus Kentucky. However, a moment of adversity became a huge step forward when Auriemma was ejected for arguing with the officials. The shocked players realized that they had to rally on their own, which they did.

Ralph and Sveta played like veterans, and Bird made sure her teammates were where they needed to be. More important than the 68–62 win was what the players proved that night, both to Auriemma and themselves. From there the team played with new focus and determination. The Huskies handled almost every team they went up against that year. Their only defeat came at the hands of (you guessed it) Tennessee. UConn split a home-and-home with the Lady Volunteers.

MARCH MADNESS AT UCONN

Entering March the team was dialed in and dedicated, to a degree that even Auriemma had not seen. The harder he pushed them, the more they seemed to say, "Is that all you've got?" In practice, he made the starters play five-on-seven because it was the only way to give them a challenge. Embodying the spirit of the Huskies was Shea Ralph, who played with such relentless energy that her teammates called her "Shea-Dog." Even with her injury history, Ralph was the first to take a charge, dive on a loose ball, or mix it up in the paint.

The 2000 postseason was special for UConn, as Auriemma's team swept through the NCAA Tournament.

In the NCAA Tournament, UConn beat Hampton by 71 points. Then came easy wins over Clemson (by 38), Oklahoma (22), LSU (15), and Penn State (22). No one could hang with the Huskies. After two seasons lost to injury, Ralph's redemption culminated in national Player of the Year honors and Final Four MVP. UConn played lockdown defense versus Tennessee in the championship game. Forward Kelly Schumacher blocked nine shots, the Lady Vols shot 31 percent and had twenty-six turnovers. The Huskies won going away, 71–52.

"There were moments during the [2000 Championship] game, I was thinking, 'This is why I worked so hard,'" Ralph said. "When we won, it was just complete elation. Just to see everyone's reactions was really cool. To see my coaches and teammates so happy, especially Coach Auriemma, because he was the reason I was able to achieve and get back [to playing]. He stuck with me and pushed me."[1]

Auriemma's high school coach, Buddy Gardler, came to the Final Four and cheered for UConn. He was there to share in the celebration. It was a reminder of how far Auriemma had come in his life. Now UConn was on top of the world again, and for the moment their always-anxious coach had nothing to worry about.

Another star would soon rise in New England. During the recruiting period, Auriemma phoned Diana "Dee" Taurasi, a phenom likely to sign with UCLA because the school was half an hour from her home. Dee was the most highly sought-after player in the nation. A rare athlete, she had large, strong hands that gave her great control over the slightly smaller women's ball—she could shoot it with a flick of the wrist, even from long range.

> "When nothing is going right, that's when you find out what kind of character you have."[2]
>
> — Geno Auriemma

As with Shea Ralph, Auriemma did not tell Taurasi what almost any other coach would: that she'd start as a freshman. As a rule Auriemma didn't start freshmen, no matter how talented they were. Taurasi chose

Connecticut because she knew she'd have to earn her playing time, competing for minutes with some of the best players in the nation. Auriemma's daughter Alysa remembers Taurasi saying this about her dad: "He builds you up before you get there, and then he just breaks you down. Then you get to January like, 'I hate this!' And then he builds you back up. So, by March? Unbeatable."[3]

"You come to Connecticut, you're the best in your class, you're on cloud nine," said Caroline Doty, who won three championships with Auriemma between 2009 and 2013. "Coach's attitude is that we're going to deflate that ego and see how great you can really be."[4]

Her first year, Dee blamed excessive turnovers on other players for not being ready to handle her no-look passes, passes often fired with the velocity of a bullet. Auriemma believes that any pass that doesn't get caught is a bad pass. Just as Sveta had to learn this lesson, Dee would as well.

At Connecticut, star players also have to commit to playing defense with the same energy and commitment as offense. In one drill, a player has to do four things before

Dailey Affirmation

In August 2017, Chris Dailey accepted the Connecticut Sun's Dydek Award, given to outstanding women who have "distinguished themselves while positively impacting the local community." Dailey is considered the glue that holds the Huskies together, handling everything from recruiting to tips on smart social media activity. "I think it's been well documented, over the years, how much CD has done for Connecticut basketball," said Auriemma. "Not just in winning and losing, but how she affects our players, on and off the court, and the example that she sets."[5]

the drill ends: contain a dribble, contest a shot, block out, and rebound the ball. Two weeks into Taurasi's freshman year she ran the drill without accomplishing those goals, and Auriemma would not let her off the hook. Finally, embarrassed and exhausted, she quit and he told her to leave. At practice the next day, no one said anything about it. Taurasi emerged from the experience a stronger player.

That year, 2000–2001, Auriemma's team was as dominant as ever. Despite a season-long slump for Ralph, the only thing that could threaten UConn's efforts to make a spirited title

While Svetlana "Sveta" Abrosimova (pictured in 1998) played with great passion, her sly sense of humor tickled Auriemma's funny bone.

defense was injury. Unfortunately, that's exactly what happened. In a game at Tennessee, Sveta Abrosimova tore a ligament in her foot. The injury ended her senior season prematurely.

Abrosimova had been saving up to fly her parents over from Russia to see her play. Donations would be an NCAA violation, but her teammates chipped in to make sure her parents could visit. After her injury, she called them and told them not to come, but they did anyway. It was a bittersweet moment for her when they arrived. Auriemma was touched when Abrosimova introduced him as her second father.

It was a sad end to the career of one of UConn's most popular players. Auriemma remembered going home to see his mother one weekend and finding a life-sized Abrosimova poster tacked on the door. There were no photos of Auriemma on display, but his mom had a giant Sveta poster.

In her absence, Ralph stepped up when the team needed her most, and Taurasi entered the starting lineup. A new rivalry was brewing, as the Notre Dame Fighting Irish would pose a major challenge for UConn that season and beyond.

FIGHTING THE IRISH

On March 6, 2001, UConn played Notre Dame in a classic, a game commemorated in Jeff Goldberg's book *Bird at the Buzzer*. In January, UConn had lost by 16 in South Bend, their biggest loss in more than a decade. By then the Big East was perhaps the toughest conference of them all, and winning the year-end tournament was a real challenge. Notre Dame was ranked No. 1 in the country, and UConn, uncharacteristically, was No. 2.

Both teams reached the Big East final in impressive fashion. There, in a game watched by a full house at Gampel and a worldwide audience on ESPN2, the players went full-throttle in an evenly matched, beautifully played game. However, the night was marred by another ACL injury for Shea Ralph when she landed awkwardly on a drive to the rim. After getting her eating disorder under control and becoming the Final Four MVP on a championship team, it was a heartbreaking end to Ralph's fifth and final year at UConn. In fact, the injury would ultimately end her playing days.

Sue Bird lifted the team's spirits by hitting a half-court bomb as the first half ended, her three-pointer giving UConn a 52–46 advantage. With the sidelined Abrosimova and Ralph cheering them on, the Huskies were determined to see something good come out of this game. Though the back-and-forth battle brought out the best in both teams, UConn would not be denied, and Bird won it with an unlikely buzzer beater.

Playing Notre Dame again in the national semifinals, senior Kelly Schumacher did her best to repeat her heroics from the previous year's championship game. She hauled in seventeen rebounds but Taurasi couldn't give the team the scoring they were missing, shooting 1-for-15 and 0-for-11 from three-point range. It would go down as the low point of her basketball career. UConn lost 90–75, and the champions were dethroned. The Fighting Irish would prove to be worthy successors, moving on to defeat Purdue for the NCAA championship.

Now seniors, the TASSK Force came into 2001–2002 on a mission. Everyone knew their roles. Like the North Carolina Tar Heels Auriemma admired, his teams don't have names on the back of their uniforms. Individual statistics take a backseat to the efficiency of the group, and this particular unit was one of the best at playing in perfect concert.

Meanwhile, Taurasi took her game to the next level. That season the Huskies posted a 35-point margin of victory, on average. Auriemma would yell things like "You guys aren't good yet!" after blowout wins. Though he thought he knew what buttons to push to coax out his team's A-game, at one point Auriemma wondered if the team would benefit from a loss, to shift the focus from going undefeated.

> "[Diana Taurasi is] probably the best women's basketball player who ever lived."[6]
>
> — Geno Auriemma

But the closest anyone could get was Virginia Tech, who lost by only nine. Tamika Williams stole two inbounds passes to salt that one away.

The team was so disciplined that year, in large part due to the leadership of Sue Bird, that Auriemma had little to do. He joked that he was being deprived of the joy of coaching because his players no longer seemed to make any mistakes.

From the beginning, Auriemma knew Diana Taurasi was in a class by herself. But he still had to help her learn how to minimize costly turnovers and fouls.

Already the team's best defender, Asjha Jones stepped up her offensive game. In the second round of the NCAA Tournament, she took over and scored 14 points in twenty-five minutes. In the semifinal she had a double double (18 points, 10 rebounds) in a blowout win over Tennessee. After finishing as the leading scorer in the Big East, Swin Cash struggled in the tournament, however, and Auriemma knew he'd need her normal competitive fire in the final versus Oklahoma. The Sooners were 32–4 and very well coached by Auriemma's friend Sherri Coale.

"White Mamba"

During Diana "Dee" Taurasi's senior year, Auriemma was asked why he was so confident that his team would win. "We got Diana, and they don't," he quipped. At UConn she won 139 of her 147 games. Kobe Bryant, whose nickname is the Black Mamba, dubbed Dee "White Mamba" for her own deadly late-game strikes. A nine-time All-WNBA player, Taurasi has led the league in scoring five times and became its all-time leading scorer in 2017. In addition to her three WNBA championships, she won four Olympic gold medals.

It was Easter time, and the team convened for a special dinner before the final game. At the end of the evening Auriemma got everyone's attention in order to make a prediction —in a hoops version of the Resurrection, Swin Cash would rise from the dead and lead UConn to the national championship. Not everyone in attendance appreciated Auriemma's riff on the Bible, but most of the players laughed, including Cash.

Against Oklahoma, Taurasi wasn't playing well but Auriemma still called a crucial play for her with about three minutes left in the game. She converted a three-point play to foul out Oklahoma's leading scorer in the game. UConn pulled away, winning their third national championship by an 82–70 score.

And Swin Cash? Cash led the team in scoring (20) and rebounds (13), shooting ten of twelve from the foul line. She was named Final Four Most Outstanding Player.

7

THREE FOR THREE

For Auriemma, the case of point guard Maria Conlon was another learning experience. She'd been a Husky for two years by the time the 2002–2003 season rolled around. Unlike other members of the team, Conlon hadn't been highly recruited and was more of a leap of faith for Auriemma. Conlon lacked confidence, perhaps because she was surrounded by so many superstars. In her freshman year Auriemma's assistant coaches told him she needed encouragement. That was the last thing he'd give her; his view was that if Conlon believed in herself and played well, *then* he would compliment her. This went on for two years.

Even in 2002–2003, when it was Conlon's turn to play after Sue Bird went on to the WNBA, Auriemma didn't provide positive feedback for her great start to the season. She came into the season in great shape and ready to lead. Consequently, the tension only built between them. It was infuriating for her, which only led Auriemma to remain stubborn about withholding praise.

Finally, Auriemma called Conlon into his office and they hashed it out in loud tones. She got him to admit that if he didn't believe in her, he wouldn't be playing her thirty-plus minutes per game! This satisfied Conlon, and Auriemma realized he'd been too stubborn for too long. "I could have saved my staff and myself a lot of trouble if I had just talked to Maria earlier," Auriemma wrote in his autobiography. "But I can't, because I am too busy being a jerk."[1]

The beef was squashed, Conlon and Auriemma became close friends, and the point guard had a UConn career that surpassed expectations. "If someone asked me, 'What's the one thing you need to improve upon as a coach?' the answer would be easy," said Auriemma. "I would say, 'I need to recognize that my stubbornness gets me in big trouble.'"[2]

THE YOUNG GUNS

Over the course of that season, UConn's winning streak continued from the undefeated 2001–2002 campaign, establishing a new record for the women's game.

Gender Equity

In 2004, UConn won the national championship in both men's and women's basketball during the same season, the first time in history that a Division I school was able to do so. The men beat Georgia Tech 82–73 and, less than twenty-four hours later, the women knocked off Tennessee 70–61. They would repeat this feat in 2014. That season marked the fourth time that both teams reached the Final Four in the same year.

Auriemma had to confront his own stubborness as he and point guard
Maria Conlon (*far left*) worked through a rocky relationship.

The streak stretched to seventy straight wins before the Huskies
finally lost in March. Auriemma wasn't bothered by this defeat
because his team had really come together. The young guns had
grown up. Whenever Taurasi or Conlon were off their game, one of
the new kids rose to the occasion. In the NCAA Tournament, UConn
needed 35 points from Taurasi to beat TCU, but in the Final Four it
was Willnett Crockett who bailed them out against Texas. Between
that game and the championship round, Conlon turned the ball over
just once. Her transformation from apprehensive bench warmer to
floor general was complete.

Going into the final against Tennessee, Auriemma wrote down
the names of the previous year's starters in the locker room. He
pointed at each name and then the player replacing her, saying that

the graduated seniors were still with them, in spirit and through all the hard-earned truths they'd passed on to their successors. Against the Vols, the Huskies played up to that lofty standard and emerged with a 73–68 win.

Having gone back-to-back as champions, the team's goal became the elusive "three-peat." In any sport it's a tall order to win consecutive titles, let alone three in a row. And while Auriemma's key players returned to Storrs in 2003–2004, this season was not a thing of beauty. Taurasi battled injuries but, unlike the year before, there wasn't someone to fill in every time she faltered. Auriemma's charges made maddening mistakes and lost games they shouldn't have.

Taurasi took it personally because as the team's resident superstar she was held responsible for everything pertaining to women's basketball at UConn, more so even than Auriemma. One day she came into his office, distraught, and he told her, "You can't hide from what you are. You are Diana Taurasi, and everyone thinks you are invincible, and you have to be onstage all the time. But that's too bad. This is how it is. Stop pouting, because no one is going to leave you alone." Meanwhile, he told her teammates what Taurasi never would—she needed them to be there for her.[3]

The satellites revolving around Taurasi's sun had realized that she couldn't shine brightly every moment of every day. At tournament

> *"I'd trust him with anything . . . He forced me to become somebody special."*[4]
>
> — **Diana Taurasi**

time—when it counted the most—the team finally clicked on all cylinders again. While Taurasi was named Most Outstanding Player, everyone had their own big moments to be proud of. Taurasi didn't have to do it alone, and with a win over Tennessee the Huskies got their three-peat. "Domination, baby," said a jubilant Taurasi after the game. "When you think of UConn, you think of domination."[5]

CLASH OF THE TITANS

Over the years, UConn's rivalry with Tennessee produced some epic games. It seemed as though UConn played Tennessee in the NCAA championship game almost every year. While that isn't the case, the two programs' histories are certainly intertwined.

After Auriemma took over as coach of the Huskies, it quickly began to seem as though he and Pat Summitt were taking turns breaking each other's hearts. Auriemma always appreciated the way Summitt handled it when it was UConn who came out on top. "When you win as much as Pat and I have won, you better learn how to accept losing, too," Auriemma said. "If you lose, the first order of business is to congratulate the people who won, and allow them to feel how they should feel—that they did something great."[6]

The rivalry spanned twelve years and twenty-two meetings. By the time UConn and Tennessee began going head-to-head twice a year in the regular season, from 2001 to 2007, the rivalry had grown heated. It stood to reason—how could teams face each other so many times, often with the highest stakes imaginable, and not develop an adversarial relationship?

Without the steel-sharpens-steel effect that it had, each team knowing it had to play its absolute best to beat the other, it's safe to assume neither program would have reached the level of basketball excellence that they did.

"For me, the most fun about it was every single game we played against them there was something at stake," said Auriemma. "Either a NCAA Tournament game, national championship or just in the minds of a lot of people. I don't know how many times we were both either one or two in the country when we played. There never was a meaningless game."[7]

Though Auriemma's relationship with Pat Summitt had its ups and downs, they both elevated the profile of women's basketball nationwide.

UConn won thirteen of the team's twenty-two meetings, including all four tussles with the NCAA title on the line. For her part, Summitt got the better of Auriemma once in the Final Four and once in the Elite Eight. She also won their final three meetings.

When Auriemma's squad played Summitt's, they put on such a show that it became must-see TV. The most viewed women's NCAA

Tournament game in ESPN's history is the 2004 national title game between UConn and Tennessee. Their clashes were consistently the most-watched women's games of the season.

Auriemma's off-the-cuff comments to the press weren't always taken well in Tennessee. Notably, he teased his good friend Harry Perretta for his close relationship with Summitt and referred to the Lady Vols as "the Evil Empire." Auriemma maintains that the latter quip was a reference to the New England vs. New York rivalry embodied by the Red Sox and Yankees, with UConn representing New England and Tennessee standing in for New York.

> *"If we didn't have to compete against each other we'd all be best friends."*[8]
>
> **— Kim Mulkey**

Summitt hailed from the gentlemanly South, while Auriemma had an East Coast edge and a pointed wit that wasn't always chivalrous. At the 2000 Final Four in Philadelphia, Auriemma joked about rival cheesesteak joints in Philly: one was called Pat's and the other Geno's. "Pat's is older and more dilapidated," he said. "Geno's is bigger and brand new."[9]

The Tennessee coach was only twenty-one months older than Auriemma, so he wasn't exactly disrespecting his elders, but Auriemma's brand of humor didn't sit well with Summitt. In her 2013 book, *Sum It Up: A Thousand and Ninety-Eight Victories, a Couple of Irrelevant Losses, and a Life in Perspective,* she wrote that "Geno always liked to make barbed remarks, but it seemed to me that

Summitt of the Sport

No college basketball coach has won more games than Pat Summitt. In her thirty-eight years at Tennessee, she never endured a losing season. But more important than her 1,098 wins and eight national championships was her impact on the game. The quality of play she conjured from her teams, game to game and season to season, increased the legitimacy of the sport. The Lady Volunteers became a brand, and Summitt herself became synonymous with women's basketball. She pushed for TV exposure, and Tennessee's excellence made viewers glad they'd tuned in. Sadly, an Alzheimer's diagnosis forced her to step down in 2012, and, four years later, Summitt died.

from 2000 on, they had an ungenerous edge. Oddly, the more success UConn had, the more Geno resented Tennessee."[10]

The bad blood got so bad that Summitt canceled the home-and-home series in 2007, soon after her school sent the SEC a letter alleging a pattern of recruiting violations at UConn. There was no doubt that the teams competed for players as well as championships, but the NCAA never took disciplinary action against UConn, even after acknowledging a "secondary violation" took place. It happened in 2006, when both Tennessee and UConn courted Georgia phenom Maya Moore. At the request of UConn, ESPN gave Moore a tour of their facility in Bristol, Connecticut, a privilege they would presumably not extend to the average high school student. Though any impact on Moore's decision is unknown, this represented a recruiting violation and prompted Summitt to pull the plug on the series.

"If we didn't have to compete against each other we'd all be best friends," said Baylor coach Kim Mulkey about the Auriemma-Summitt feud. "I think sports and competition bring out the best and the worst in all of us…Feuds happen because of competition."[11]

Despite the personality conflict and hardwood heavyweight fights, Auriemma made an effort to patch things up with Summitt moments after UConn defeated Tennessee to win the 2004 national championship. "Don't listen to all this crap you hear and read," he said. "Sometimes I just say things for fun. It's not meant to be at your expense. I have tremendous respect for what you've done, and how you do it, and that will always be true."[12]

Auriemma was also among the first to donate to the Pat Summitt Foundation to fight Alzheimer's. "He wrote out a check on the spot—for $10,000," Summitt wrote in her book.[13]

Auriemma has said that while he and Summitt were very different, he respected her for what she did for the women's game. After her death he posted on his team's Facebook page. "Coach Summitt defined greatness and set the bar for the rest of the sport," he said. "Thank you for the greatest games, the fiercest rivalry, and for the inspiration for success. Rest in Peace, Coach."[14]

8

A GOLDEN AGE

After Diana Taurasi put a triumphant exclamation point on her UConn career, the program needed the next generation to come of age before the Huskies would return to the elite. Still, they made the Sweet Sixteen in 2004–2005 and Elite Eight the next two seasons, going a remarkable 89–17 over that span. By 2007–2008 the team was again poised for greatness.

Freshman phenom Maya Moore was a true

> *"Competitive greatness, John Wooden used to say, was being at your best when your best was needed."*[1]
>
> — Geno Auriemma

do-it-all player with such athleticism she dunked publically at sixteen years old. Moore helped her high school team win three Georgia state titles and one national championship. With the Huskies, she broke several freshman records in a 36–2 season.

That year UConn beat Big East rival Rutgers to advance to the Final Four, where they'd have a rematch with Stanford in the national

In Maya Moore, Auriemma found Diana Taurasi's successor and a player whose prodigious all-around game could carry the team when needed.

semifinals. The Huskies prevailed in the first meeting but now they were without two starters, Mel Thomas and Kalana Greene. Stanford jumped out to a lead but UConn rallied, closing the deficit to 47–46. Then Stanford's Candice Wiggins went off, drilling consecutive three-pointers to spark a 10–0 run. The disappointed Huskies would not advance to face Tennessee in yet-another national championship tilt. Summitt's Lady Vols beat Stanford for the title.

After the Stanford loss, Moore went into her head coach's office. "She goes, 'I just realized I can't do this,'" Auriemma remembered.

"I said, 'Really? You just realized this is five-on-five?' Maya had to learn how to play with four other really good players on her team, because Maya always wanted to do everything by herself and win it by herself." [2]

COMING OUT OF THE COLD

The Huskies carried this stinging disappointment into the next season and came out loaded for bear in 2008–2009. They were ranked No. 1 in both major preseason polls, by nearly unanimous votes (Tennessee and Stanford received a single vote each). The team returned most of its core players, including team leader Renee Montgomery, and added highly regarded freshmen Caroline Doty, Tiffany Hayes, and Heather Buck.

Auriemma's squad stormed out of the gates with one win after another, including a 32-point victory over No. 4 Oklahoma. It became clear that another undefeated season might be in the offing. Maya Moore scored 40 against Syracuse, becoming the second player in UConn history to break the 40-point mark

Maya's Empire

Maya Moore went 150–4 at UConn, becoming the program's all-time leading scorer and the first Division I women's basketball player to amass 2,500 points, 1,000 rebounds, 500 assists, 250 steals, and 150 blocked shots. Her 2010–2011 season was honored with every major individual award. Moore was more than a hardwood heroine—she graduated from UConn with a 3.7 GPA. The Minnesota Lynx made her the first overall pick in the 2011 WNBA draft. She is a four-time WNBA champion and two-time Olympic gold medalist.

(Nykesha Sales did it in 1997). That season Moore led the team in scoring, rebounding (tying with Tina Charles), and steals. She was second in assists and fell three short of the team lead in blocked shots. The super-soph claimed every possible National Player of the Year award.

Before facing their old foes, Notre Dame, in February, the Huskies had trailed for a combined twenty-seven minutes all season. In this one, though, the Irish led for most of the first half and early in the second. Then UConn's 43–41 deficit turned into a 10-point win, their narrowest victory of the season. The team emerged from the Big East Tournament 30–0, with an eye on the national championship trophy.

Moore averaged a team-high 22 points per game during UConn's march through the NCAA Tournament. With the consistency of a metronome, the Huskies maintained their steady drumbeat of excellence. Nothing makes that point more clearly than the identical 83–64 scores they posted in defeating Arizona State and Stanford to reach the program's sixth NCAA championship game. At first, Louisville limited Moore and Renee Montgomery. But Tina Charles took charge under the basket, pacing the team with 25 points and 19 boards in a 76–54 win.

Amazingly, no team had managed to lose to UConn by less than ten points, let alone beat them, in their perfect 39–0 season. This set a new, difficult-to-break record. "When you're on long [winning] streaks, he knows what to focus on," Moore said of Auriemma. "At that point, it's about distractions. It's the only thing that's going to

Maya Moore has been called the greatest winner in the history of women's basketball. Her trophy case includes two NCAA titles, two Olympic gold medals, four WNBA rings, and three WCBA championships.

mess you up. Your team is the best. The thing that's going to knock you off is distractions. He was a master of helping us with that."[3]

Unbelievably, UConn was even better the next season. The Huskies again finished the regular season undefeated, this time posting an average margin of victory of 35.9 points. Until the NCAA Tournament, the team's closest contest came against Stanford—in that one, the winning margin was a mere 12 points.

At tournament time, Moore and Charles played little more than half the minutes of each game, until the Final Four. There, led by freshman Brittney Griner, Baylor hung with the Huskies and only trailed 41–38 with fifteen minutes to go. Even in her first season Griner was a shot blocker extraordinaire. Despite Griner's heroics, Auriemma and company won by 20.

The team that gave them the most trouble in the regular season, Stanford, would do so again in the national championship game. The Cardinal held the Huskies to 12 points in the first half, the lowest total in the history of women's basketball at the University of Connecticut. To say that 20–12 was a shocking halftime score would be an understatement.

It was all slipping away—a seventy-seven-game winning streak, a perfect season, and back-to-back championships. But there was no panic in the locker room. Auriemma didn't need to give this group a stirring pep talk. Maya Moore told the press after the game that she

Brittney's Block Party

Before Brittney Griner, dunks were rare in the women's game— but not anymore. She equaled Candace Parker's career record (two) in her first WNBA game. Griner's great "hops" help her as a shot-blocker, as well; Griner owns records in that category, too. At Baylor, she set the all-time single-season record for blocks, as a *freshman*. As a junior, she blocked more shots than any Division I *team*. In 2017, Griner added another feather in her cap, leading the WNBA in scoring.

knew "it couldn't get any worse" than a 12-point half. There was "no fear" in this team, she said. "We knew a run was coming. We settled down and hit some big shots."[4]

In the second half Moore hit a very big one herself, a momentum-shifting three-pointer, to give UConn a 23–22 lead. The team then went on a 30–6 run to win, 53–47. "It's what great players do," Auriemma said. "They do it at the most pressure-packed times—that makes them who they are."[5]

Entering 2010–2011 on a seventy-eight-game unbeaten streak, UConn needed only eleven more wins to break the record set by John Wooden's UCLA men's team in the 1970s. But Tina Charles and Kalana Charles had graduated, while Caroline Doty would miss the whole year with a knee injury. Though the record was broken, the streak ended at ninety when Stanford defeated the Huskies. The Cardinal had handed UConn its last defeat, 998 days earlier, in the 2008 Final Four. To put the Huskies' achievement into perspective, they went more than 142 weeks without losing a game. During the streak UConn trailed for only 134 minutes, and of that time only 13 minutes were in the second half of games.

Auriemma got the team back on track, and UConn completed the regular season without losing again. In the Final Four, the Huskies faced Notre Dame for the fourth time that season. This time the Fighting Irish prevailed, despite a 36-point outburst from Maya Moore. There would be no three-peat. Still, Moore would

Auriemma coached a number of former Huskies on the US women's national team. The 2012 team, pictured here, struck gold at the Summer Olympics in London.

bring Auriemma's teachings with her into the WNBA, where her success continued.

Sometime before she graduated, Auriemma gave her a framed quote on the subject of perfection. "Admire it, aspire to it, but don't require it."[6] Moore said she had already committed the words to memory.

GETTING THE BAND BACK TOGETHER

Auriemma had always been interested in coaching the US women's national team, but the timing wasn't right until 2009. Then, under his tutelage, former Huskies Sue Bird, Swin Cash, Diana Taurasi, Maya Moore, and Tina Charles joined forces with Angel McCoughtry,

Lindsay Whalen, and other WNBA stars to win gold at the 2010 World Championships and 2012 Summer Olympics.

"Managing this—the stress level here—is hard," Auriemma said of Olympic competition. "Really hard. Just because it's USA Basketball. At Connecticut, if the season ends in April and it doesn't go your way, next November you start the season back up again and everybody gets the

> *"Maya's a great scorer, and you get that reputation by scoring points under pressure. She certainly did that."*[7]
>
> **— Geno Auriemma**

chance to be born again. If this doesn't end well this weekend it's four more years you have to wait to get back here. That's unacceptable. There's not enough wine on that boat."[8]

Auriemma reprised his role as head coach for the 2014 FIBA World Championship and the 2016 Summer Olympics in Rio, this time with UConn's Breanna Stewart in the fold. In the final Taurasi and Whalen scored 17 points apiece in a 101–72 victory over Spain. The win marked the fourth straight gold medal presentation for Taurasi and Bird. Auriemma's team won their eight games by an average margin of 37.3 points, a very "UConn" accomplishment.

9

FOUR-PEAT?!

- - - - - - - - - - - - - - -

The next big surge in UConn's fortunes came in 2012–2013, when the recruiting class yielded Breanna Stewart, the top recruit in the nation; Morgan Tuck, a two-time Illinois Ms. Basketball; and blazingly fast point guard Moriah Jefferson. Stewart was a particularly marvelous player, causing constant mismatches with her size and freakishly diverse skill set, and this trio would later go first, second, and third in the 2016 WNBA draft.

Stewart openly proclaimed that she planned to win four titles in her time in Storrs. "Once you openly say it nationally," Dailey said, "then you give us [as coaches] the permission to say, 'OK, Stewie, that's what you really want to do? Then we're going to show you this is how you're going to have to operate to give yourself that chance.'"[1]

GROWING PAINS

There were growing pains, of course. In Stewart's freshman year she heard Auriemma yell "Get in your stance!" so many times it might as well have been her name. Stewart was capable of eye-popping plays, but she frustrated Auriemma with her seemingly lackadaisical stretches in practice. She explained that she was used to saving much of her energy for games. Auriemma, of course, wants games to feel like a breeze compared to his practices. "A lot of times her freshman year, she wanted it to be easy," Auriemma said. "When it wasn't, she couldn't deal with it. Now she's the first one to talk about, 'Hey, this is going to be hard, but we've got it.'" [2]

As he had with the superstars who came before her, Auriemma would hammer away at Stewart with critiques of little things he saw on film, things he didn't always come down on her teammates for. "My big thing with my great players is that you're not playing against the other team," said Auriemma. "The other team is irrelevant. You're playing against the game itself. How much does that mean to you that you want to master the game?" [3]

Stewart, Tuck, and Jefferson grew up together, as players, but there were bumps in the road as the Huskies were beaten by Notre Dame (twice) and Baylor. Any defeat is notable in a UConn season, and the loss to Baylor was

Can't Stop "Stewie"

"She's intense, but in her own way," Auriemma said of Stewart. "So she'll turn it on and then dial it back. She's not overly concerned with numbers. She's not like Diana [Taurasi] yet, ready to paint a new masterpiece on the canvas every night for six months. But the bigger the game, the better she plays." [4] After being selected first overall by the Seattle Storm, where she joined former UConn star Sue Bird, Stewart won WNBA Rookie of the Year honors in a landslide vote. She is already a two-time Olympic gold medalist.

In Breanna Stewart, the Huskies found their next superstar. Stewart credits
Auriemma with pushing her to unlock her full potential as a player.

Stewart's worst game ever. Auriemma went so far as to speculate that the Huskies may have won if he hadn't played her. Then, in the Big East tournament, Notre Dame beat UConn yet again. These were close losses, but they caused Auriemma angst nonetheless.

He needn't have worried. The team raised their level of play in the NCAA Tournament, avenging the loss to Notre Dame in the Final Four before blowing out Louisville 93–60. Auriemma secured his eighth national championship, tying the record set by Pat Summitt. The next generation had delivered immediately, so there would be no disruption of team continuity with the changing of the guard. Just how good could this class be, in four years together?

The answer was very, very, very good.

The Big East dissolved at the end of that season, separating Notre Dame and UConn to put a damper on another contentious rivalry. From April 2011 to March 2013, Notre Dame won seven out of its eight meetings with UConn, a feat no team but Tennessee has accomplished in the Geno Auriemma era.

> "I had to be pushed to a level that I didn't know I could play at."[5]
> — Breanna Stewart

It certainly didn't hurt the Huskies' winning percentage to get away from Notre Dame, as in the 2013–2014 season UConn beat every opponent by at least ten points and easily reached the NCAA Tournament final, where they faced… Notre Dame. The Irish were also undefeated, marking the first time two unbeaten teams had squared off for the championship. But Notre

By her senior year, Breanna Stewart no longer needed much coaching to play at the highest level—she had internalized everything Auriemma wanted to teach her.

Dame was missing one of its top players, Natalie Achonwa, who tore her ACL in the Elite Eight. UConn prevailed, 79–58, to complete a 40–0 season.

By this point "Stewie" was perhaps the best all-around player the game had seen. A unique talent, she is a dominant low-post player but uses her length at six-foot-four to shoot over defenders on the perimeter. "I had to be pushed to a level that I didn't know I could play at,"[6] Stewart said. Here was a player living up to her fullest potential, and Auriemma's tough love had a lot to do with it.

In 2014–2015, the Huskies set their sights on a third consecutive title. After an early stumble vs. Stanford, in overtime, they reeled off another thirty-seven straight wins. The national championship game was a rematch, but the outcome was the same. UConn again defeated Notre Dame, this time by a 63–53 score. The three-peat was complete.

HOOPS HISTORY IS MADE

Stewart and the class of 2012 were seniors in 2015–2016, at the height of their powers and poised to become top-ten draft picks in the WNBA. UConn also added the nation's top prospect, shooter Katie Lou Samuelson, who became a rare freshman starter for Auriemma.

About halfway through the season, Auriemma stopped talking to Stewart. She later figured out that he did this so that complacency wouldn't set in with a nearly flawless player. Auriemma said that he often stops coaching seniors because soon enough, they won't have him around to motivate them anymore. "You should be tired of looking to me to get your inner strength," he said. "It's gotta come from you. Because now, once you look in the mirror and go, 'OK, I need to do this,' then you know that's never going away. If you get it from me, it might go away."[7]

This squad was as dominant as any Auriemma had ever assembled. Their victory margin was 39.7 points en route to an undefeated season and an 82–51 romp over Syracuse in the championship game. UConn was the first women's basketball team to win four straight NCAA Division I titles, and the feat has only been accomplished once in the men's game. Stewart became the first player to be named Final Four Most Outstanding Player in all four seasons of her college career. Her versatility was also unmatched—Stewart is the only player in Division I history to top 300 in both assists and blocks, two statistics that very few players can produce in tandem.

Auriemma has said that Stewart made the biggest impact in her NCAA Tournament appearances of any player to come through the hallowed halls of UConn. When called upon, she always rose to the occasion. "I'll say this," Auriemma said. "She's the greatest NCAA Tournament player I've ever been around. When the lights were the brightest, that's (when) she was at her best."[8]

The 2012 class won more games than anyone in the history of college basketball, and their four championships is also unprecedented. "There's

> *"I trust him, that was one of the main reasons I came here."* [9]
>
> — **Katie Lou Samuelson**

three key ingredients that go into this kind of success, 'One, two, three,'"[10] Auriemma said after the championship game, pointing to his three seniors (Stewart, Tuck, and Jefferson).

Auriemma's eleventh championship set a new record for a college basketball coach, surpassing UCLA's "Wizard of Westwood," the legendary John Wooden. Wooden was the only other coach to win four straight college hoops titles in Division I (1967–73).

"What those eleven championships mean to me is how many great players I've had the opportunity to coach," said Auriemma. "How many great people have come through the program. It doesn't matter whose name is above, or whose name I'm under. As long as I have those players in my memory, I'm good."[11]

10

LEADERSHIP AND LOYALTY

E ven with a largely new cast of characters wearing navy and white, the team's winning streak reached epic proportions in the 2016–2017 season. With a win over SMU, UConn broke its own record of ninety-one straight. The streak came to a dramatic end in the 2017 NCAA Tournament, where Mississippi State's Morgan William hit a game winner in overtime to upset the unbeaten Huskies and put an end to talk of the "five-peat."

UCONN LOSES IT

They can't win them all, even if sometimes it seems like they do. Geno Auriemma's UConn Huskies have become something bigger than a basketball team. They're like a Broadway play that is such a big hit it goes on tour, playing to a packed house in every city. The team has set countless road attendance records at different schools. "There

In the wake of UConn's 2017 NCAA Tournament loss to Mississippi State, even Geno Auriemma was briefly at a loss for words.

did come a point where everybody wanted to see us," Auriemma said. "Everybody wanted us to come to their building, every TV event wanted us to be a part of it. Young programs wanted Connecticut to come to their building so they could test themselves. It got to the point where our kids looked forward to that." [1]

How can Auriemma top four straight championships and a 111-game winning streak? It seems impossible, but maybe no goal is too lofty for the UConn women's basketball team. By spring 2018, they had eleven NCAA titles, six undefeated seasons, and eleven consecutive Final Fours. Auriemma had the highest winning percentage among NCAA basketball coaches at any level, men's or women's (.880) and seems destined to top Pat Summitt's tally for career wins.

With another talented roster, this one led by offensive powerhouse Katie Lou Samuelson, the team will surely contend for more titles in the years to come. Still, in characteristic fashion, Auriemma has his concerns. "It's getting much, much harder to connect with every kid on the team in the way that you need to, that they need you to," said Auriemma. [2]

For all of his achievements, Auriemma will also be remembered for his controversies. In media circles he was blasted for conspiring with his friend, Villanova head coach Harry Perretta, to arrange a layup for Nykesha Sales so she could break UConn's career scoring record on a torn Achilles', an act seen by some as an inauthentic achievement and a violation of the spirit of competition. Then there was the time Auriemma took heat for snapping at a UConn student-newspaper reporter, live on ESPN, when she asked him a question he didn't appreciate.

And Auriemma will be the first to admit he's hard on his players. Extremely. "It's hard to pick out

Record-Breaking Bruins

Winning ten championships, John Wooden's Bruins were one of the greatest dynasties in the history of sports. Auriemma grew up as a UCLA fan and admired the unparalleled greatness of Wooden's 1971–74 squads. He remains uncomfortable being compared to the "Wizard of Westwood," whose enduring win streak Auriemma bettered in 2010. President Barack Obama called Auriemma to congratulate him, saying, "It's a great thing for sports." [3]

girls who can handle Geno's toughness," said Shea Ralph. "It's hard to play here. Geno's always pushing you. We don't play girls' basketball, we play basketball."[4]

How do other Husky alums feel about Auriemma and his badgering style? Did it alienate them? "I've covered countless

> *"I don't coach women. I coach basketball players."*[5]
>
> — Geno Auriemma

basketball teams, both male and female, college and professional, and in almost twenty-five years as a sports journalist I have never—ever—encountered a group of athletes who are so fiercely protective of their coach as this one," said Jackie MacMullan, coauthor of Auriemma's autobiography.[6]

Part of the reason for that is the fact that for all his bluster, Auriemma wears his emotions, and his vulnerabilities, on his sleeve. He's not ashamed to admit it when he feels anxious or in over his head. His outsider's insecurities are obvious and something many people can relate to without being an immigrant from a poor family who works in an industry where your gender is an issue for some.

Another reason ex-Huskies so vigorously defend Auriemma is that they know they meant more to him as people than as players. When Auriemma's former player and assistant coach Jamelle Elliott lost her father, he paid for funeral arrangements and ensured that every member of the team got to Washington, DC, for the service. He rearranged the team's schedule so that Sue Bird's mother could host a dinner for the team the first time Bird went home as a Husky.

No matter how many championships UConn wins, Auriemma is just as motivated as ever—each trophy honors the players for all the sacrifices they've made since they first set foot in Storrs.

Auriemma never cashed a check from Meghan Pattyson to repay a $1,000 loan to help her get through lean times. He cordoned off an area of the stands so Rebecca Lobo's mother could watch her play without threatening an immune system weakened by cancer. These are some of the reasons why Auriemma's players remain close to him, long after their cap-and-gown ceremonies.

COACHING IS CARING

Auriemma offered to work for free in 2017–2018 to stave off steep budget cuts at UConn. He's always been willing to help other members of the coaching profession, whether it's teaching an assistant the intricacies of the triangle offense or giving Sherri Coale advice and support in her first year as the coach of the Oklahoma Sooners. A number of Auriemma's ex-players have become coaches, including Jen Rizzotti, Jamelle Elliott, Tamika Williams, Shea Ralph, Paige Sauer, Stacy Hansmeyer, Carla Berube, Wendy Davis, and Tonya Cardoza.

Before every game, the Huskies join hands in the center of the locker room and yell, "Together!" That unity of purpose, intent, and dedication is a powerful thing. Talented players long to be a part of it and have trouble letting it go. So, too, does Auriemma. Retirement is not a word he has openly contemplated. Now that he's found a measure of serenity, he's enjoying coaching more than ever.

"As I've gotten older, I've learned that I'm on a run right now," Auriemma said in 2016. "I'm on a big run like at the casino where you go and play blackjack and it just keeps going your way, and keeps going your way, and you know if you stay there long enough, it's going to turn. I know that. But while I'm on

> *"We've won a lot of national championships, and we've never taken any of them for granted."[7]*
>
> — Geno Auriemma

this run, I've learned you can't control it all, so just try to control the things that you can and let it go. I had a real hard time in my young coaching career doing that, and I've just gotten really good at it."[8]

Auriemma may have evolved over the years, but has he really learned to "let it go"? Maybe, maybe not, but two things never change. Though his players agree that it's absolutely worth it, he remains a hard coach to play for. And blue moons are more common than his losses.

Kathy Auriemma doesn't know when Geno's run is going to end. "He is going to do this until something else makes him think, 'Wow, that would be fascinating,'" she said. "Nothing [else] has drawn him… There's going to be a purpose about what he does next, whether it's retire and not do anything, or whatever. That's not here yet."[9]

"I have the best job in the world," said Auriemma. "But what's the next thing I need to know to get to the next level? I feel there's so much out there I don't know. Things I haven't seen."[10]

Auriemma has been giving us things we haven't seen from the moment he got to UConn, so perhaps it is his turn to have that pleasure. Until he's good and ready, though, the win streaks will roll on.

CHRONOLOGY

- -

1954 Luigi "Geno" Auriemma is born in Montella, Italy.

1972 While attending Montgomery County Junior College, Geno meets his future wife, Kathy.

1978 Auriemma becomes an assistant coach at St. Joseph's University, working under women's coach Jim Foster.

1981 Auriemma joins Debbie Ryan's coaching staff at the University of Virginia.

1985 The University of Connecticut hires Auriemma to coach their women's basketball team.

1989 The Huskies make their first-ever appearance in the NCAA Tournament.

1991 Rebecca Lobo is the first elite national recruit to play for UConn.

1995 Auriemma coaches the Huskies to the NCAA championship, defeating Tennessee

2000 UConn beats Tennessee to win its second national title.

2002 The Huskies prevail against Oklahoma in the NCAA championship game.

2003 UConn goes "back-to-back," defeating Tennessee in the NCAA final.

2004 To complete the three-peat, the Huskies knock off Tennessee once again.

2006 Auriemma is elected to the Naismith Memorial Basketball Hall of Fame and the Women's Basketball Hall of Fame.

2007 Auriemma is inducted into the National Italian American Sports Hall of Fame.

2009 Auriemma wins his sixth national championship when UConn defeats Louisville.

2010 Stanford stays close but UConn wins its second straight NCAA title.

2012 Auriemma coaches the US Olympic team to a gold medal at the London Games. He also receives the John R. Wooden Legends of Coaching Award.

2013 A new dynasty begins as Breanna Stewart and the Huskies dispatch Louisville.

2014 UConn beats Notre Dame in the national championship game.

2015 Notre Dame loses the rematch as the Huskies win their third straight title.

2016 UConn wins a blowout over Syracuse to complete the four-peat, winning Auriemma's eleventh NCAA championship. He wins several coach of the year awards, including the Naismith College Coach of the Year.

2017 The Huskies' NCAA record-winning streak is snapped at 111 straight games. Auriemma once again wins several more coach of the year awards, including the Naismith Coach of the Year.

2018 The Huskies make the NCAA Final Four for the nineteenth time with Auriemma as their coach.

CHAPTER NOTES

- - - - - - - - - - - - -

INTRODUCTION

1. Geno Auriemma and Jackie MacMullan, *Geno: In Pursuit of Perfection* (New York, NY: Grand Central Publishing, 2009), p. 171.

2. Sherri Coale, "Geno's Voice Always Strikes Right Tone," ESPN.com, February 3, 2015, http://www.espn.com/womens-college-basketball/ story/_/id/12271259/connecticut-huskies-coach-geno-auriemma-voice-always-strikes-right-tone.

3. Pat Jordan, "Geno Auriemma, Mr. Women's Basketball," Deadspin, March 22, 2012, https://deadspin.com/5895516/ geno-auriemma-mr-womens-basketball.

4. Jeff Goldberg, *Bird at the Buzzer: UConn, Notre Dame, and a Women's Basketball Classic* (Lincoln, NE: University of Nebraska Press, 2013), p. 49.

5. Ibid, p. 55.

6. Auriemma and MacMullan, p. 20.

7. Ibid, p. 85.

8. Ibid, p. 2.

CHAPTER 1: FORGING A WORK ETHIC

1. Geno Auriemma and Jackie MacMullan, *Geno: In Pursuit of Perfection* (New York, NY: Grand Central Publishing, 2009), p. 1.

2. Pat Jordan, "Geno Auriemma, Mr. Women's Basketball," Deadspin, March 22, 2012, https://deadspin.com/5895516/geno-auriemma-mr-womens-basketball.

3. Auriemma and MacMullan, p. 3.

4. Jeff Jacobs, "Think UConn's Geno Auriemma Is A Rock? You Should Meet His Wife," *Hartford Courant*, April 1, 2016, http://www.courant.com/sports/uconn-womens-basketball/hc-jacobs-column-0401-20160331-column.html.

5. Auriemma and MacMullan, p. 176.

6. MaryEllen Fillo, "Welcome to the House Geno AND Kathy Auriemma Built," *Hartford Courant*, March 29, 2015, http://www.courant.com/java/hc-fillo-kathy-auriemma-0329-20150327-story.html.

7. Ibid.

8. Geno Auriemma, http://www.azquotes.com/quote/581062.

9. Jim Shea, *Huskymania: The Inside Story of the Rise of the UConn's Men's and Women's Basketball Teams* (New York, NY: Villard, 1995), p. 187.

CHAPTER 2: NO WARM WELCOME IN STORRS

1. Jim Shea, *Huskymania: The Inside Story of the Rise of the UConn's Men's and Women's Basketball Teams* (New York, NY: Villard, 1995), p. 17.

2. Yes Network, "University of Connecticut women's basketball coach Geno Auriemma takes CenterStage," October 23, 2015, http://web.yesnetwork.com/news/article.jsp?ymd=20151023&content_id=155354582&fext=.jsp&vkey=news_milb.

3. Geno Auriemma, http://www.genoauriemma.com/geno/quotes/.

4. Shea, p. 19.

5. Ibid, p. 24.

6. Ibid, p. 223.

7. Geno Auriemma and Jackie MacMullan, *Geno: In Pursuit of Perfection* (New York, NY: Grand Central Publishing, 2009), p. 30.

8. Ibid, p. 31.

9. Shea, p. 136.

10. Geno Auriemma, http://www.genoauriemma.com/geno/quotes/.

11. Auriemma and MacMullan, p. 36.

CHAPTER 3: CHEMISTRY TESTS

1. Jim Shea, *Huskymania: The Inside Story of the Rise of the UConn's Men's and Women's Basketball Teams* (New York, NY: Villard, 1995), p. 138

2. Geno Auriemma, http://www.azquotes.com/author/23306-Geno_Auriemma.

3. Shea, p. 140.

4. Geno Auriemma and Jackie MacMullan, *Geno: In Pursuit of Perfection* (New York, NY: Grand Central Publishing, 2009), p. 144.

5. Shea, p. 174.

6. Shea, p. 143.

7. "Rebecca Lobo Career Retrospective," NBA.com, September 8, 2017, http://www.nba.com/video/2017/09/08/career-retrospective-hall-fame-rebecca-lobo?collection=video/mustseehighlights.

8. Shea, p. 174.

9. Ibid, p. 205.

10. Julie Foudy, "Kathy Auriemma Plays Key Role in UConn's Storied Success," ESPN.com, http://www.espn.com/espnw/video/19038101/kathy-auriemma-plays-key-role-uconn-storied-success.

11. Pat Jordan, "Geno Auriemma, Mr. Women's Basketball," Deadspin, March 22, 2012, https://deadspin.com/5895516/geno-auriemma-mr-womens-basketball.

CHAPTER 4: THE PURSUIT OF PERFECTION

1. Jim Shea, *Huskymania: The Inside Story of the Rise of the UConn's Men's and Women's Basketball Teams* (New York, NY: Villard, 1995), p. 150.

2. Ibid, p. 151.

3. Ibid, p. 206.

4. Ibid.

5. Jeff Goldberg, *Bird at the Buzzer: UConn, Notre Dame, and a Women's Basketball Classic* (Lincoln, NE: University of Nebraska Press, 2013), p. 92.

6. Shea, p. 155.

7. Ibid, p. 4.

8. Ibid, p. 156.

9. Geno Auriemma, https://www.inspiringquotes.us/quotes/9HzU_5dBTqkVL.

10. Shea, p. 10.

11. Ibid, p. 163.

12. Ibid, p. 10.

13. Rebecca Lobo, "Hall of Fame Ceremony: Rebecca Lobo Speech," NBA.com, September 8, 2017, http://www.nba.com/video/2017/09/08/201709 08-hall-fame-ceremony-rebecca-lobo-speech.

14. Shea, p. 164.

CHAPTER 5: GROWTH SPURTS

1. Jim Shea, *Huskymania: The Inside Story of the Rise of the UConn's Men's and Women's Basketball Teams* (New York, NY: Villard, 1995), p. 13.

2. Gene Wang, "Before Jennifer Rizzotti Joined Geno Auriemma's Coaching Tree, She Stood Up to Him," *Washington Post*, December 20, 2016, https://www.washingtonpost.com/sports/colleges/before-jennifer-rizzotti-joined-geno-auriemmas-coaching-tree-she-stood-up-to-him/2016/12/20/2a72c926-c6d3-11e6-85b5-76616a33048d_story.html?utm_term=.74f47887e486.

3. Shea, 190.

4. Geno Auriemma and Jackie MacMullan, *Geno: In Pursuit of Perfection* (New York, NY: Grand Central Publishing, 2009), p. 77.

5. Ibid, p. 85.

6. Ibid.

7. Ibid, p. 121.

8. Jeff Goldberg, *Bird at the Buzzer: UConn, Notre Dame, and a Women's Basketball Classic* (Lincoln, NE: University of Nebraska Press, 2013), p. 6.

CHAPTER 6: THE RESURRECTION

1. Jeff Goldberg, *Bird at the Buzzer: UConn, Notre Dame, and a Women's Basketball Classic* (Lincoln, NE: University of Nebraska Press, 2013), p. 36.

2. Geno Auriemma and Jackie MacMullan, *Geno: In Pursuit of Perfection* (New York, NY: Grand Central Publishing, 2009), p. 126.

3. Paul Doyle, "As Chris Dailey Prepares for Honor, Love Pours in from UConn Family," *Hartford Courant*, August 7, 2017, http://www.courant.com/sports/uconn-womens-basketball/hc-uconn-women-chris-dailey-0808-20170807-story.html.

4. Alysa Auriemma, "Watching My Dad Coach Women's Basketball Helped Me Become a Feminist," ESPN.com, February 9, 2017, "http://www.espn.com/espnw/voices/article/18647289/watching-my-dad-coach-women-basketball-helped-become-feminist.

5. Harvey Araton, "Breanna Stewart, UConn's Wow Factor, Always Had a Sweep in Mind," *New York Times*, February 28, 2016, https://www.nytimes.com/2016/02/28/sports/ncaabasketball/breanna-stewart-uconns-wow-factor-always-had-a-sweep-in-mind.html?_r=0.

6. Auriemma and MacMullan, p. 46.

CHAPTER 7: THREE FOR THREE

1. Geno Auriemma and Jackie MacMullan, *Geno: In Pursuit of Perfection* (New York, NY: Grand Central Publishing, 2009), p. 230.

2. Ibid.

3. Ibid, p. 261.

4. Ibid, p. xiv, p. xv.

5. Staff, "UConn Men and Women Both Won National Titles 10 Years Ago," *New Haven Register*, April 3, 2014, http://www.nhregister. com/uconn/article/UConn-men-and-women-both-won-national-titles-10-11385121.php.

6. Auriemma and MacMullan, p. 131.

7. Jeff Jacobs, "To Geno, Nobody Means More to Women's Basketball Than Summit," Hartford Courant, June 28, 2016, http://www.courant. com/sports/uconn-womens-basketball/hc-jacobs-column-geno-auriemma-pat-summitt-0628-20160627-column.html.

8. Jason Whitlock, "Whitlock 1-on-1," https://www.youtube.com/ watch?v=ZCKa4J4-abY.

9. Erik Brady, "As Tennessee Legend Pat Summitt Is Memorialized, a Rivalry Is Remembered," *USAToday*, July 7, 2016, https://www.usato-day.com/story/sports/ncaaw/2016/07/07/pat-summitt-tennessee-geno-auriemma-connecticut-rivalry/86814942/_.

10. Pat Summit and Sally Jenkins, *Sum It Up* (New York, NY: Crown Archetype, 2013), p. 327.

11. Whitlock.

12. Auriemma and MacMullan, p. 285.

13. Summit and Jenkins, p. 329.

14. Rebecca Greenberg, "Geno Auriemma Reflects on Pat Summitt's Death," WWLP.com, June 28, 2016, http://wwlp.com/2016/06/28/geno-auriemma-reflects-on-pat-summitts-death/.

CHAPTER 8: A GOLDEN AGE

1. Don Amore, "Connecticut Breaks UCLA record with 89th Straight Vctory," *Los Angeles Times*, December 21, 2010, http://articles.latimes.com/2010/dec/21/sports/la-spw-uconn-basketball-20101222.

2. Mechelle Voepel, "Taurasi, not Stewart, Largely Considered Best UConn Player Ever," ESPN.com, April 5, 2016, http://www.espn.com/womens-college-basketball/story/_/id/15133875/is-breanna-stewart-diana-taurasi-maya-moore-greatest-player-connecticut-huskies-history.

3. Jeff Zillgitt, "Olympic Women's Basketball Coach Geno Auriemma Wins and Is Expected to Win," *USAToday*, August 17, 2016, https://www.usatoday.com/story/sports/olympics/rio-2016/2016/08/17/geno-auriemma-usa-basketball-uconn-gold-medal-ncaa-championships/88912284/.

4. Doug Feinberg, "Connecticut Beats Stanford 53-47 for NCAA title," *San Diego Union Tribune*, April 6, 2010, http://www.sandiegouniontribune.com/sdut-connecticut-beats-stanford-53-47-for-ncaa-title-2010apr06-story.html.

5. Ibid.

6. Elizabeth Merrill, "Being Breanna Stewart," ESPN.com, March 29, 2016, http://www.espn.com/espn/feature/story/_/page/espnw-stewart160329/how-breanna-stewart-leading-uconn-huskies-fourth-straight-national-title.

7. Ibid.

8. Zillgitt.

CHAPTER 9: FOUR-PEAT?!

1. Mechelle Voepel, "Huskies Aren't Burdened by Pressure in Pursuit of Four-peat," ABC News, April 5, 2016, http://abcnews.go.com/Sports/huskies-burdened-pressure-pursuit-peat/story?id=38166602.

2. Harvey Araton, "Breanna Stewart, UConn's Wow Factor, Always Had a Sweep in Mind," *New York Times*, February 28, 2016, https://www.nytimes.com/2016/02/28/sports/ncaabasketball/breanna-stewart-uconns-wow-factor-always-had-a-sweep-in-mind.html?_r=0.

3. Mechelle Voepel, "Taurasi, not Stewart, Largely Considered Best UConn Player Ever," ESPN.com, April 5, 2016, http://www.espn.com/womens-college-basketball/story/_/id/15133875/is-breanna-stewart-diana-taurasi-maya-moore-greatest-player-connecticut-huskies-history.

4. Elizabeth Merrill, "Being Breanna Stewart," ESPN.com, March 29, 2016, http://www.espn.com/espn/feature/story/_/page/espnw-stewart160329/how-breanna-stewart-leading-uconn-huskies-fourth-straight-national-title.

5. Ibid.

6. Ibid.

7. Ibid.

8. Doug Feinberg, "UConn Rolls to 4th Consecutive National Title Behind Stewart," AP News, April 6, 2016, https://apnews.com/588fcf67fe434078a92ab57ab920b869/uconn-rolls-4th-consecutive-national-title-behind-stewart.

9. Howard Megdal, "Case for UConn's Geno Auriemma Being Best Coach Ever Goes Beyond Basketball," CBSSports.com, March 8, 2017, https://www.cbssports.com/college-basketball/news/case-for-uconns-geno-auriemma-being-best-coach-ever-goes-beyond-basketball/.

10. Feinberg.

11. Ibid.

CHAPTER 10: LEADERSHIP AND LOYALTY

1. Jeff Goldberg, *Bird at the Buzzer: UConn, Notre Dame and a Women's Basketball Classic* (Lincoln, NE: University of Nebraska Press, 2013), p. 50.

2. Sue Favor, "Is Geno Auriemma Preparing to Retire?" Women's Hoops World, April 7, 2016, http://womenshoopsworld.com/2016/04/07/is-geno-auriemma-preparing-to-retire/.

3. Don Amore, "Connecticut Breaks UCLA Record with 89th Straight Victory," *Los Angeles Times*, December 21, 2010, http://articles.latimes.com/2010/dec/21/sports/la-spw-uconn-basketball-20101222.

4. Pat Jordan, "Geno Auriemma, Mr. Women's Basketball," Deadspin, March 22, 2012, https://deadspin.com/5895516/geno-auriemma-mr-womens-basketball.

5. Ibid.

6. Geno Auriemma and Jackie MacMullan, *Geno: In Pursuit of Perfection* (New York, NY: Grand Central Publishing, 2009), p. 299.

7. Geno Auriemma, http://www.genoauriemma.com/geno/quotes/.

8. Jeff Zillgitt, "Olympic Women's Basketball Coach Geno Auriemma Wins and Is Expected to Win," *USAToday*, August 17, 2016, https://

www.usatoday.com/story/sports/olympics/rio-2016/2016/08/17/
geno-auriemma-usa-basketball-uconn-gold-medal-ncaa-champion-
ships/88912284/.

9. Jordan.

10. Ibid.

GLOSSARY

ACL Anterior cruciate ligament. When torn, this knee ligament requires a lengthy healing and recovery period.

bench-warmer Slang for a member of the team who does not receive much playing time.

bigs Slang for a basketball team's front court players—the center and forwards.

buzzer beater A shot made as time expires on the clock, often to win a game.

Division I The highest level of intercollegiate athletics sanctioned by the NCAA.

double double Achieved when a player totals ten of two different statistics, such as points and rebounds.

field goal A basket scored on any shot other than a free throw; worth either two or three points depending on the distance of the attempt.

Final Four The national semifinals of the NCAA Tournament, when only four teams remain in contention for the championship.

NCAA National Collegiate Athletic Association, the governing body for college sports.

point guard The position generally responsible for running the offense and distributing the ball to teammates on the offensive side of the court.

rebound The statistic associated with securing a missed shot after the ball hits the rim of the basket.

roster The list of players on a team and available to play in a game.

seed In a tournament, the ranking that determines who a team or competitor plays first. Typically, the purpose of seeding is to separate favorites to win the tournament for as long as possible.

triangle offense A strategy popularized by coach Tex Winter that forms a triangle shape through the spacing of players on the floor and passes the ball from point to point in order to obtain an easy shot.

turnover When a player loses possession of the ball to the other team.

FURTHER READING

- - - - - - - - - - - - - - - -

BOOKS

Auriemma, Geno, with Jackie MacMullan. *Geno: In Pursuit of Perfection*. New York, NY: Grand Central Publishing, 2010.

Davis, Seth. *Getting to Us: How Great Coaches Make Great Teams*. New York, NY: Penguin Press, 2018.

Goldberg, Jeff. *Bird at the Buzzer: UConn, Notre Dame, and a Women's Basketball Classic*. Lincoln, NE: University of Nebraska Press, 2013.

WEBSITES

GenoAuriemma.com

www.genoauriemma.com/geno/biography

Learn about the coach's life and ventures, including his forays into wine, spaghetti sauce, and restaurants.

UConnHuskies.com

www.uconnhuskies.com/sports/w-baskbl/conn-w-baskbl-body.html
Get an inside look at the UConn Huskies, with interviews, news, game previews, and more.

FILM

UConn: The March to Madness. HBO, 2017.

INDEX